B-25 Mitchell

Written by David Doyle

In Action

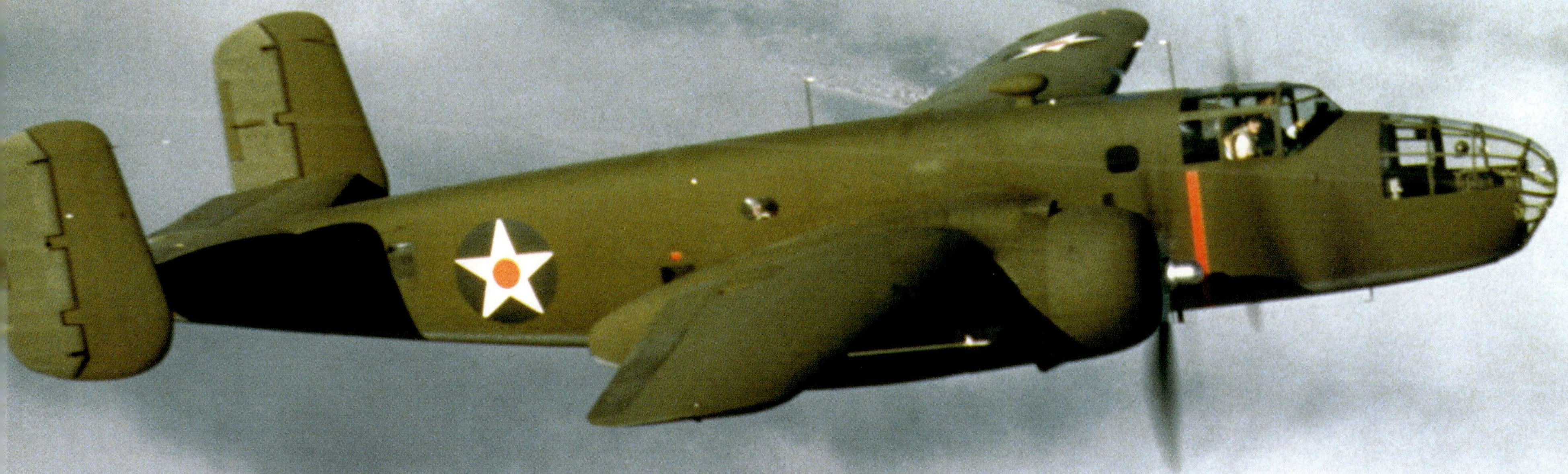

Cover Art by Don Greer

Line Illustrations by Melinda Turnage

(Front Cover) The B-25 gained immortality on 18 April 1942 when sixteen B-25Bs under Lt. Col. Jimmy Doolittle took off from the deck of the USS *Hornet* and executed a surprise attack on military targets on the Japanese island of Honshu, including some in Tokyo.

(Back Cover) The B-25J-30 44-30934 with its gun nose exemplified the late-war Mitchell. *Betty's Dream* served with the 499th Bomb Squadron, 345th Bomb Group in the Philippines. It flew escort for the Japanese peace envoys to the surrender conference in Manila on 19 August 1945, and also on the 21 August return trip.

About the In Action® Series

In Action® books, despite the title of the genre, are books that trace the development of a single type of aircraft, armored vehicle, or ship from prototype to the final production variant. Experimental or "one-off" variants can also be included. Our first *In Action®* book was printed in 1971.

ISBN 978-0-89747-625-6

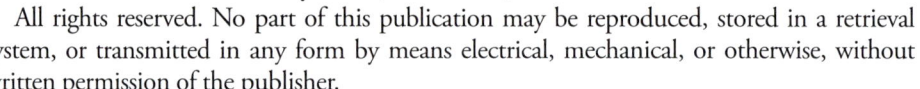

Proudly printed in the U.S.A.
Copyright 2011 Squadron/Signal Publications
1115 Crowley Drive, Carrollton, TX 75006-1312 U.S.A.

All rights reserved. No part of this publication may be reproduced, stored in a retrieval system, or transmitted in any form by means electrical, mechanical, or otherwise, without written permission of the publisher.

Military/Combat Photographs and Snapshots

If you have any photos of aircraft, armor, soldiers, or ships of any nation, particularly wartime snapshots, why not share them with us and help make Squadron/Signal's books all the more interesting and complete in the future? Any photograph sent to us will be copied and returned. Electronic images are preferred. The donor will be fully credited for any photos used. Please send them to:

Squadron/Signal Publications
1115 Crowley Drive
Carrollton, TX 75006-1312 U.S.A.
www.SquadronSignalPublications.com

(Title Page) The North American B-25 Mitchell was one of the premier U.S. warplanes of World War II. The absence of a top turret on this B-25B is possibly due to a delay in the delivery of the Bendix turrets in mid-1941. (Stan Piet collection)

Dedication

As with all of my projects, this book would not have been possible without the generous help of many friends – some old, some new. Specifically, Tom Kailbourn; Stan Piet; Brett Stolle and the staff of the National Museum of the United States Air Force; the staff and volunteers at the National Museum of Naval Aviation, the staff of the National Archives; the Dyersburg Army Air Base Memorial Association (DAABMA); and the estate of PFC Alexander R. Zaboly, 488th Bombardment Squadron, 340th Bomber Group. The editorial team at Squadron Publications, led by Chuck Harransky, bent over backwards to help with this project, and are instrumental in its completion. This work could not have been done without the unflagging support of my wife Denise, and our boys Andrew and Brandon.

Introduction

America's most famous medium bomber of World War II was the B-25 Mitchell. No small measure of its fame is derived from the daring attack on Japan by 16 of these aircraft led by Lt. Col. Jimmy Doolittle in April 1942. For this raid, the aircraft carrier *Hornet* not only launched the raid on Tokyo, but also catapulted the B-25 to glory.

The B-25 was dubbed the Mitchell, honoring General William L. "Billy" Mitchell, who is recognized as the father of strategic bombing, and who, as early as 1924, predicted a coming war with Japan in which Pearl Harbor, Hawaii, would be the target of an airborne attack. It was a fitting coincidence that the bomber bearing his name be used for the Tokyo raid. Not only did the attack, just four months after the shock of Pearl Harbor, boost U.S. morale, but it was also strategically significant, as it forced Japan to divert war materiel for home-island defense.

As we shall see, however, the plane that took part in this raid, the model B-25B, was not the most potent of the Mitchells.

The lineage of the B-25 can be traced back to North American Aviation's model NA-40, itself an outgrowth of the earlier NA-21 and NA-39. The NA-40 was built privately by North American to be a contender in the Army Air Corps light attack bomber bidding. Following the replacement of the original Pratt & Whitney engines with Wrights, the NA-40 was redesignated NA-40B. But after the NA-40B was lost in a crash during testing on 11 April 1939, Douglas was awarded the attack bomber contract and produced the A-20 Havoc. Far from throwing in the towel on its NA-40, however, North American was just beginning its development.

The immediate forerunner of the B-25 was North American Aviation's NA-40, designed and manufactured entirely at North American's expense as a result of the U.S. Army Air Corps call for proposals for a twin-engine medium bomber on 18 January 1938. The shape of the bombardier's greenhouse, the tricycle landing gear, and the twin vertical tails would carry over to the North American B-25. The sole NA-40 enjoyed a flying career of only five weeks before it was destroyed in a crash on 11 April 1939. First equipped with Pratt & Whitney R-1830 engines, the NA-40 was redesignated NA-40B after being refitted with Wright R-2600-71 engines. (National Museum of the United States Air Force)

The NA-40B's engine cowls exhibit less tapered profiles than those of the NA-40. With its Wright engines and streamlined cowlings, the NA-40B performed significantly better than the NA-40. Despite the very brief testing career of the NA-40B, sufficient data were accumulated to satisfy North American that the design was sound. (National Museum of the United States Air Force)

Visible on the vertical stabilizer is the NA-40B's civil registration number, X14221. Armament of the NA-40B consisted of .30-caliber machine guns, with one in a ball mounted in the clear nose, one in the blister-type turret on the top of the aircraft, a moveable one that could be positioned in the waist or ventral windows, and two fixed guns in each wing. (National Museum of the United States Air Force)

B-25 Mitchell Development

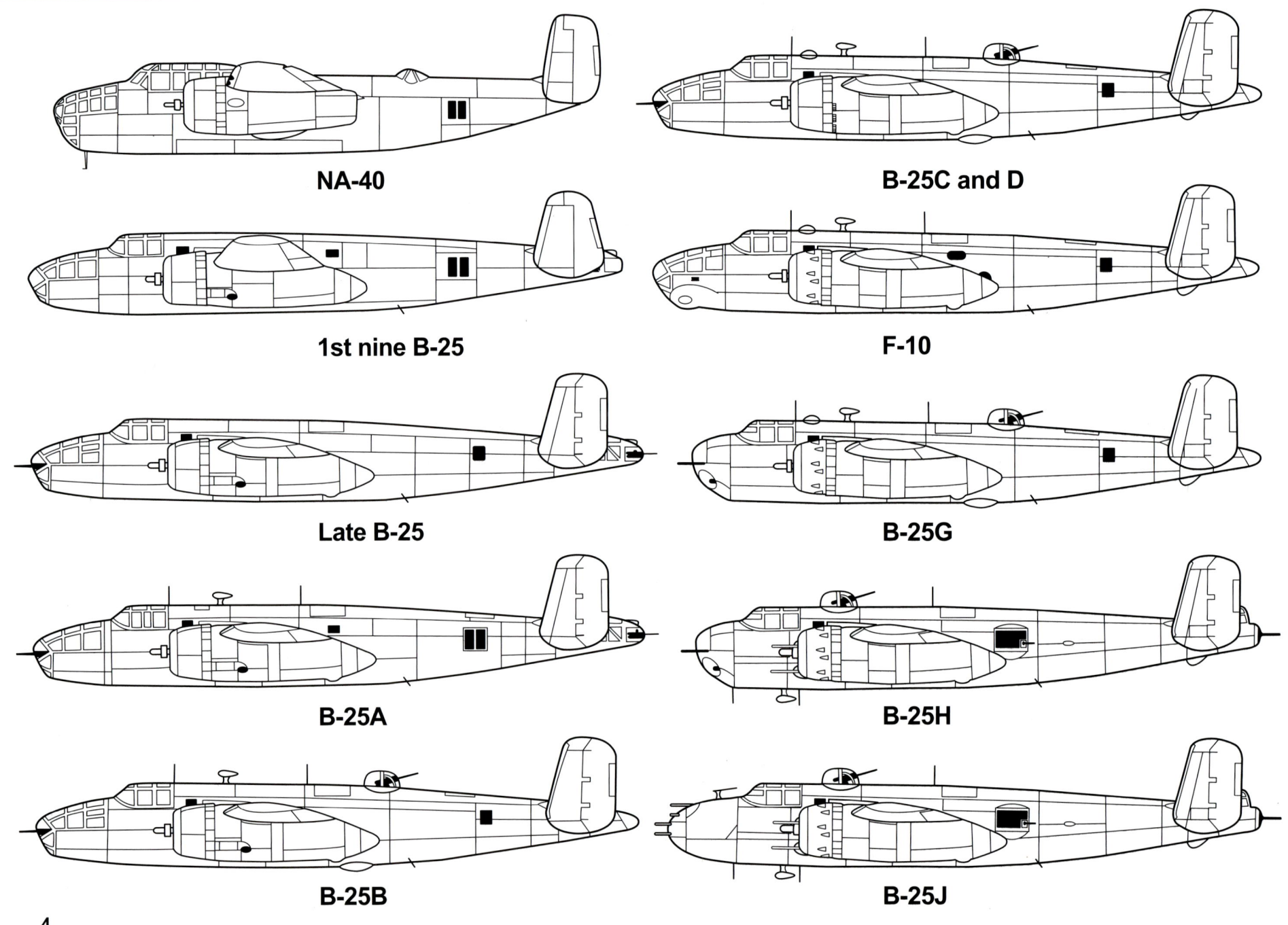

B-25

Using some of the design elements of the NA-40, North American produced the Model NA-62 in response to the Air Corps' revised proposal No. 39-640 for a medium bomber, dated 11 March 1939. Five months later, the Air Corps contracted for 184 of these aircraft, redesignating the first 24 examples the B-25. This aircraft featured mid-fuselage-mounted wings with engine nacelles mounted under them, an upper fuselage deck that extended back from the top rear of the cockpit canopy, and twin vertical tails. (National Museum of the United States Air Force)

B-25

One month to the day prior to the crash of the NA-40B, the Army had requested proposals for a medium bomber. Pleased overall with the performance of the NA-40, North American's engineers, led by Lee Atwood, revamped the design, giving it the model number NA-62. The NA-62 strongly resembled the NA-40, but was somewhat larger, in order to accommodate the 3,000-pound bomb load specified by the Air Corps (vs. 2,100 pounds for the NA-40). The NA-62 was 54.2 feet long, whereas the length of the NA-40 was 47.8 feet. The NA-62 had a 67.5-foot wingspan (vs. 66 feet for the NA-40); and was 16.3 feet high, (vs. 15 feet). The fuselage was widened, allowing the pilots to sit side by side, rather than in tandem as on the NA-40. Gross weight rose from the NA-40's 19,741 pounds to 28,577. On 10 August 1939 the Army ordered 184 of the model NA-62, even before the first one had flown. North American's NA-62 was designated the B-25.

The winds of war in Europe brought about expedited procurement of the new aircraft, and the usual experimental X-aircraft and service-test Y-aircraft were dispensed with. The new bomber went straight into production.

Because of this accelerated program, several running changes were made, the most notable being a modification in the wing geometry after nine aircraft had been completed. Initially the wing of the B-25 had a constant dihedral of slightly more than four degrees. Beginning with the tenth B-25, the dihedral outboard of the engines was reduced to zero degrees, 21 minutes 39 seconds, giving the bomber the slight gull-wing appearance that it would retain throughout production.

The number-one B-25 was photographed at Mines Field, California, in August 1940. Early B-25s were delivered in bare-metal finish, with red and white horizontal stripes and blue vertical stripes on the tails. The crew comprised the pilot, copilot, bombardier, navigator/radio operator, and gunner. There was no crew armor, and armament was limited to three .30-caliber machine guns in flexible mounts in the nose, floor, and waist, and a .50-caliber machine gun in the tail. (National Museum of the United States Air Force)

As seen in this photo of the number-one B-25, the first nine B-25s were built with constant wing dihedral, meaning the wings had the same angle with reference to the vertical centerline of the aircraft from wing root to wing tip. Because this configuration resulted in instability in flight, the last 14 B-25s were delivered with the dihedral eliminated from the outer wing sections. The engines were Wright R-2600-9 Cyclones, with 14 cylinders arranged in two tiers. (National Museum of the United States Air Force)

Several vertical tails were tried on the number-one B-25, including one with a nearly rectangular shape with rounded corners and the smaller, tapering units seen in this photograph. The vertical tails finally adopted for subsequent models of the B-25 had a straight, vertical trailing edge. A good view of the early tail turret is available, with its clear panels set in a rather complex frame. The retractable tail skid would remain a feature of B-25s until the B-25C model. (National Museum of the United States Air Force)

In this rear view of one of the first nine B-25s, the constant wing dihedral is visible. The twin vertical tails were parallel with each other. When the main landing gear was lowered, the main landing gear doors remained closed: only the small doors visible inboard of the landing gear struts remained open. (National Museum of the United States Air Force)

Early B-25s lacked a top turret, having instead a top window opening in the radio operator's compartment through which a .30-caliber machine gun could be fired. Above the rear of the engine nacelle is the side window of the radio compartment. Protruding from the leading edge of the right wing is the pitot tube. (National Museum of the United States Air Force)

At the very rear of the tail turret are two clamshell doors made of Plexiglas. When the .50-caliber machine gun was mounted in this position, its barrel pushed either door open as the gun was traversed from side to side. Visible below the right vertical tail is the waist window, consisting of two clear panels in a frame. (National Museum of the United States Air Force)

One of the first nine B-25s appears in a two-tone camouflage scheme of olive drab on the top and side surfaces and neutral gray on the lower surfaces. The vertical tails are of the final design, with sloping leading edges on the vertical stabilizers, and vertical trailing edges on the rudders. (National Museum of the United States Air Force)

This view of an early B-25 emphasizes the constant wing dihedral as well as the shape of the tail turret. To operate the tail machine gun, the gunner could sit, kneel, or lie down. On top of the fuselage between the wings is the football-shaped housing for the automatic direction finder (ADF) antenna. (National Museum of the United States Air Force)

Beginning with the 10th B-25, the wings were redesigned, with the sections outboard of the engine nacelles having no dihedral. This feature gave the wings somewhat of the appearance of an inverted gull wing. The wide stance of the main landing gear struts is apparent; the landing gear was hydraulically operated. (National Museum of the United States Air Force)

The 10th production B-25 is seen in flight. The low-lying clear canopy of the tail turret is visible at the rear of the fuselage. The vertical line extending down the fuselage from the rear side window of the cockpit was a red warning symbol, cautioning crewmen on the ground to stay clear of the spinning propellers. (National Museum of the United States Air Force)

The U.S. Army Air Corps is conducting static load tests on this B-25. It is suspended in a frame rigged with weight scales, and weight-calibrated sandbags are neatly stacked on the wings to test their ability to withstand loads. It was in this position that the wings finally failed. Extra sandbags are stacked up on the floor in the foreground. (National Museum of the United States Air Force)

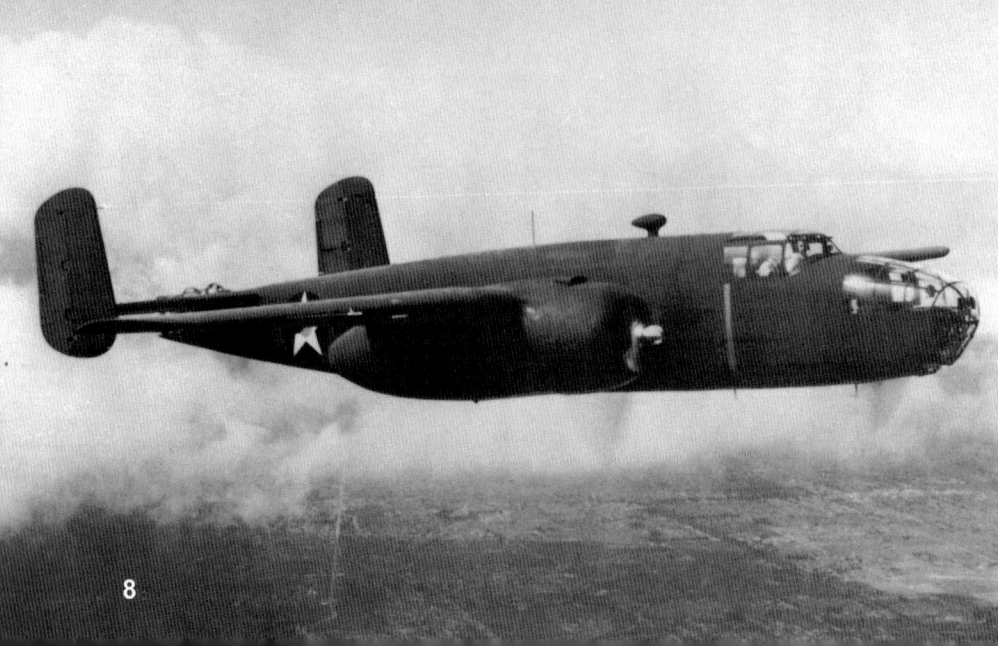

B-25A

This B-25A bears the Thunderbird insignia of the 34th Bomb Squadron of the 17th Bomb Group, tail markings 17B for 17th Bomb Group, and 43, the aircraft's individual number. The B-25A represented aircraft numbers 25 to 64 of U.S. Army Air Corps contract No. W535-ac-13258 of 20 September 1939, of which the B-25 had comprised the first 24 examples built. The B-25A was essentially identical to late B-25s, with the addition of armor plating for crewmembers and self-sealing fuel tanks. (Air Force Historical Research Agency)

As the U.S. military and aeronautical firms studied the unfolding air war in Europe and sought to learn from Allied combat experience, North American worked to turn its model NA-62A, the B-25A, into a more combat-fit aircraft.

While the new model was outwardly identical to the 15 final B-25s built, internally the B-25A held many improvements. Foremost among these modifications was the addition of armor protection for the bomber's crew. Seat backs for the pilot, co-pilot, and bombardier were protected by 3/8-inch armor plate, as was the bottom of the bombardier's position. The tail and waist gunners also were provided with armor protection.

No less important, beginning with the 25th B-25A, self-sealing fuel tanks began to be installed. While this change reduced the bomber's fuel capacity from 912 to 694 gallons and cut the aircraft's range from 2,000 to 1,350 miles, the reduced hazard of fire and explosion was significant. To counter this reduced fuel capacity, critical on long ferry flights, provisions were made for the installation of a 418-gallon tank in the bomb bay. These tanks were also sometimes installed in aircraft used for patrol. All of these changes pushed the weight of the late B-25A up 1,000-pounds over that of the B-25.

The B-25A flew for the first time on 25 February 1941 with Ed Virgin at the controls. Forty of the type were produced, bearing serial numbers 40-2189 through 40-2228. These aircraft, like the B-25 and the subsequent B-25B, were all part of the initial 20 September 1939 Army contract AC-13258 for 184 NA-62 bombers plus one test airframe.

Despite these improvements, even after the United States entered WWII, no B-25A was deployed overseas. The first unit equipped with the B-25A was the 17th Bomb Group at McChord Field in Washington state. The type was also supplied to the 30th Bomb Group based in New Orleans, Louisiana; the 39th Bomb Group in Spokane, Washington; the 43rd Bomb Group in Bangor, Maine; and the 44th Bomb Group at McDill Field, Florida.

A gunner mans the .50-caliber machine gun in this close-up of a B-25A tail turret. The gun rests on a bright metal frame called an adapter, which contained a shock-buffering mechanism and also incorporated hand grips for moving the gun. The pivoting clamshell doors, made of Plexiglas, are here closed around the barrel of the gun, but would swing open as the machine gun was traversed from side to side.

B-25 Mitchell Data

	B-25	B-25A	B-25B	B-25C	B-25D	B-25G	B-25H	B-25J
Armament:	3 x .30 cal. + 1 x .50 cal.	3 x .30 cal. + 1 x .50 cal.	4 x .50 cal.	4 x .50 cal.	4 x .50 cal.	1 x 75mm + 12 x .50 cal.	1 x 75mm + 6 x .50 cal.	variable
Bomb load:	3,000 lbs.	3,000 lbs.	3,000 lbs.	3,200 lbs.	3,200 lbs.	3,200 lbs.	3,000 lbs.	3,000 lbs.
Engines (2):	Wright R-2600-9; 1,700 h.p.	Wright R-2600-9; 1,700 h.p.	Wright R-2600-9; 1,700 h.p.	Wright R-2600-13; 1,700 h.p.	Wright R-2600-13; 1,700 h.p.	Wright R-2600-13; 1,700 h.p.	Wright R-2600-13; 1,700 h.p.	Wright R-2600-29; 1,700 h.p.
Maximum speed:	322 mph @ 15,000 ft.	315 mph @ 15,000 ft.	300 mph @ 15,000 ft.	284 mph @ 15,000 ft.	284 mph @ 15,000 ft.	281 mph @ 15,000 ft.	275 mph @ 13,000 ft.	293 mph @ 13,850 ft.
First flight	19 August 1940	25 February 1941	April or May 1941	9 November 1941	3 January 1942	22 October 1942	15 May 1943	3 March 1943
Service ceiling:	30,000 feet	27,000 feet	23,500 feet	21,200 feet	21,200 feet	24,300 feet	24,800 feet	24,500 feet
Range:	2,000 miles	1,350 miles	1,300 miles	1,525 miles	1,525 miles	1,535 miles	1,350 miles	1,350 miles
Wing span:	67 ft. 6 ¾ in.	67 ft. 6 ¾ in.	67 ft. 6 ¾ in.	67 ft. 6 ¾ in.	67 ft. 6 ¾ in.	67 ft. 6 ¾ in.	67 ft. 6 ¾ in.	67 ft. 6 ¾ in.
Length:	54 ft. 1 in.	54 ft. 1 in.	53 feet	53 feet	53 ft.	50 ft. 10 in.	50 ft. 10 in.	53 ft. 5 ¾ in.
Height:	15 ft. 9 in.	15 ft. 9 in.	15 ft 9 in.	15 ft. 9 in.	15 ft. 9 in.	16 ft. 4 ¼ in.	16 ft. 4 ¼ in.	16 ft. 4 ¼ in.
Maximum takeoff weight:	28,557 lbs.	27,100 lbs.	28,460 lbs.	33,500 lbs.	33,500 lbs.	33,500 lbs.	33,500 lbs.	33,400 lbs.
Number built/converted:	24	40	120	1,625	2,290	400 + 69 modified / test	1,000	4,318

This B-25A is assigned to the 17th Bomb Group, 34th Bomb Squadron, and is based at McChord Army Air Field, Washington. The 17th Bomb Group was tasked with flying coastal patrol missions in the continental United States. This aircraft bore serial number 40-2212. Serial numbers of the B-25As ranged from 40-2189 to 40-2228. (National Museum of the United States Air Force)

A B-25A, number 41 in the 34th Bomb Squadron, bears the Thunderbird insignia below the cockpit. The first air group to be fully outfitted with B-25As, the 17th Bomb Group flew these aircraft on antisubmarine patrols in the Pacific Northwest beginning in the spring of 1941. Later, the 34th Bomb Squadron would train crews for the Doolittle Raid. (National Museum of the United States Air Force)

Crewmen of the 2nd Bomb Group, which briefly flew B-25s in 1942, rush from a Jeep to their B-25A in preparation for an antisubmarine patrol mission on the East Coast in early 1942. In this early stage of B-25 antisubmarine operations, spotting enemy subs was accomplished primarily through visual sightings rather than radar. (Air Force Historical Research Agency)

Crewmen of a B-25A of the 2nd Bomb Group pose next to their aircraft in early 1942. They wear several types of leather flight trousers and a mix of flying jackets, including the A-2 and B-3 types. Several of the jackets bear a squadron insignia that appears to feature a picture of Mighty Mouse. All five crewmen wear radio headphone sets. (Air Force Historical Research Agency)

Crewmen prepare a B-25 of the 2nd Bomb Group for an antisubmarine patrol mission on the East Coast of the United States. The cowls are painted matte white, and the bomber bears the U.S. national insignia with the red circle in the center that would be eliminated from U.S. Army Air Forces insignia by orders dated 15 May 1942. At left is an L-1 Truck, Oil Servicing, 660 gallon, 2½-ton, 4x4. The truck was built by Autocar, and the tank by Heil. Trucks such as this, and later 2½-ton models, were widely used on airfields to fill the large oil reservoirs required by radial engines. (Air Force Historical Research Agency)

The B-25A was externally identical to the last fifteen B-25 aircraft, but internally the B-25A boasted self-sealing fuel tanks and armor protection for the crew. The overhead window of the radio compartment is faintly visible in this view of a B-25A. This machine gun position provided extremely limited defensive cover: basically, a cone extending above and slightly to the rear of the window. On the next model of the aircraft, the B-25B, a powered gun turret would occupy this position. (National Archives)

On 25 July 1941, this B-25A, serial number 40-2223, assigned to the 12th Reconnaissance Squadron, crashed in a landing accident at Geiger Field, Washington. The pilot was Quentin T. Quick. (National Museum of the United States Air Force)

Propeller damage on B-25A, serial number 40-2223, suggests that the engines were stopped when it crashed. Access panels have been removed from the wing, probably for inspection of engine components. (National Museum of the United States Air Force)

The crash of 40-2223 tore out the bottom of the left engine nacelle, shoving the main landing gear wheel back behind the wing. Prominent atop the fuselage is the ADF "football" antenna housing. (National Museum of the United States Air Force)

One blade of the the left propeller of B-25A, 40-2223, is bent and another is missing some of its matte black paint. Visible inside the cockpit is a seat cushion stenciled "U.S. Air Corps." (National Museum of the United States Air Force)

B-25B

New B-25Bs in olive drab and neutral gray camouflage are lined up on a tarmac. The vertical red stripe below the cockpit side window served as a visual warning to avoid the spinning propeller. Although it was planned that the B-25B feature upper and lower power gun turrets, production problems at Bendix forced several aircraft to be completed without turrets. Because of the intended turret installations, the B-25B did not feature the rear gun position as found on previous models. (USAF)

Based on its keen observation of aerial warfare over Europe, the Army Air Corps soon began to suspect that the Mitchell was ill-equipped to defend itself against enemy interceptors. The Army therefore decided to increase the protection of the remaining 120 bombers on order.

North American's engineers created their NA-62B, the B-25B, by adding Bendix power-operated turrets. Feeling that the addition of an upper and lower turret, each armed with twin .50-caliber machine guns, gave the bomber adequate firepower, the engineers deleted the rear gun position, as well as the radio-operator's upper and waist guns.

The model A4 upper turret, with its Plexiglas enclosure for weapons and operator, occupied the location of the previously installed upper window and machine gun mount. The Bendix model A5 lower turret was retractable, and was operated from inside the aircraft by a gunner using a periscope. This method was eventually determined to be ineffective, but not until production of the B-25G model was underway. One other distinguishing characteristic of the B-25B was the fact that the exhaust stack of the right engine was substantially shorter than that of the left.

It was modified B-25Bs that flew from the deck of the *Hornet* into history on 18 April 1942. Doolittle's aircraft were provided with greatly increased fuel capacity, a modification that forced the removal of the lower gun turret. Lacking rear armament, wooden dowels were installed to simulate the appearance of a rear gun position.

Of the 120 B-25B bombers built, the fifteenth crashed prior to delivery. Twenty-three were delivered to the Royal Air Force, which designated the aircraft the Mitchell I. Two B-25Bs were sent to the Soviet Union (and were presumably joined by a third, when one of the Doolittle raiders' aircraft was interned after landing near Vladivostok).

The B-25B represented a major upgrade in the defensive armaments of the Mitchell medium bomber, featuring new upper and lower turrets in the waist compartment. The top turret was enclosed in Plexiglas, and its twin .50-caliber machine guns were manned by a gunner inside the turret, while the bottom, retractable turret was operated by a gunner situated above the turret using a periscopic gun sight. (National Museum of the United States Air Force)

A B-25B of 17th Bomb Group, 95th Bomb Squadron, bears cross markings signifying the force it served with during war games in September 1941. The camouflage scheme is olive drab over neutral gray, and the front of the cowl is painted yellow. The aircraft number, 13, and 17B, signifying the 17th Bomb Group, are painted in black. The machine guns were dismounted from the turret and the bombardier's nose.

16

The top and retracted bottom turrets of a B-25B are shown close-up from the left side. The additional drag caused by the turrets cut the maximum speed by 15 miles per hour as compared with the B-25A. The cooling jackets of the top .50-caliber guns have early-type elongated slots. Oblong observation windows above the lower turret were new features of the B-25B. (National Museum of the United States Air Force)

In the overall layout of the B-25B the navigator's scanning window is immediately aft of the cockpit, and to the rear of that is the ADF 'football' antenna. Midway between the wing and tail surfaces is the top turret. The clear shot directly aft is plainly visible, but equally evident is the narrow field of fire afforded by the tail surfaces. This limitation would cause the manned tail gun position to be reinstated on later models.

The bottom turret is shown lowered. The gunner knelt above the turret in a static position facing to the rear and aimed the guns using a periscope and hand controls: an awkward arrangement that could induce vertigo in the gunner. The large window between the guns was the elevation compensator access window. The smaller window below it was the window for the periscopic gun sight.

When the bottom turret of a B-25B was in the retracted position, the lower part of the turret housing bulges slightly below the fuselage. The machine guns rest well up in the two troughs in the underside of the fuselage. The turret was electrically operated, with provisions for emergency manual operation. Two ammunition boxes within the turret housing fed the guns.

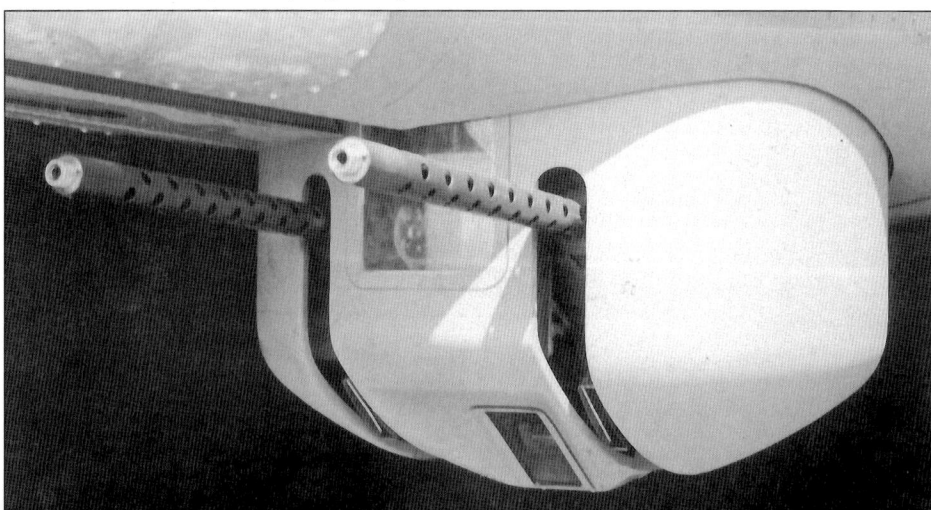 

The Doolittle raid of 18 April 1942 was designed to boost American morale in the early days of World War II by striking a daring blow against the Japanese homeland. Because of its performance characteristics and bomb load, the B-25B was selected as the attack aircraft. The carrier USS *Hornet* would carry 16 Mitchells to striking distance from the Japanese main island of Honshu. (National Museum of the United States Air Force)

Space on the flight deck of the USS *Hornet* was at a premium. This B-25B is lashed to the flush-mounted tie-down strips on the deck, with the rear of its fuselage and its empennage hanging over the fantail. Protruding from the side of the engine nacelle is the exhaust that included a heat exchanger; the right engine exhaust was shorter. (National Museum of the United States Air Force)

The *Ruptured Duck* was one of 16 B-25Bs used in the Tokyo raid on April 18, 1942. It was flown by Lt. Ted W. Lawson.

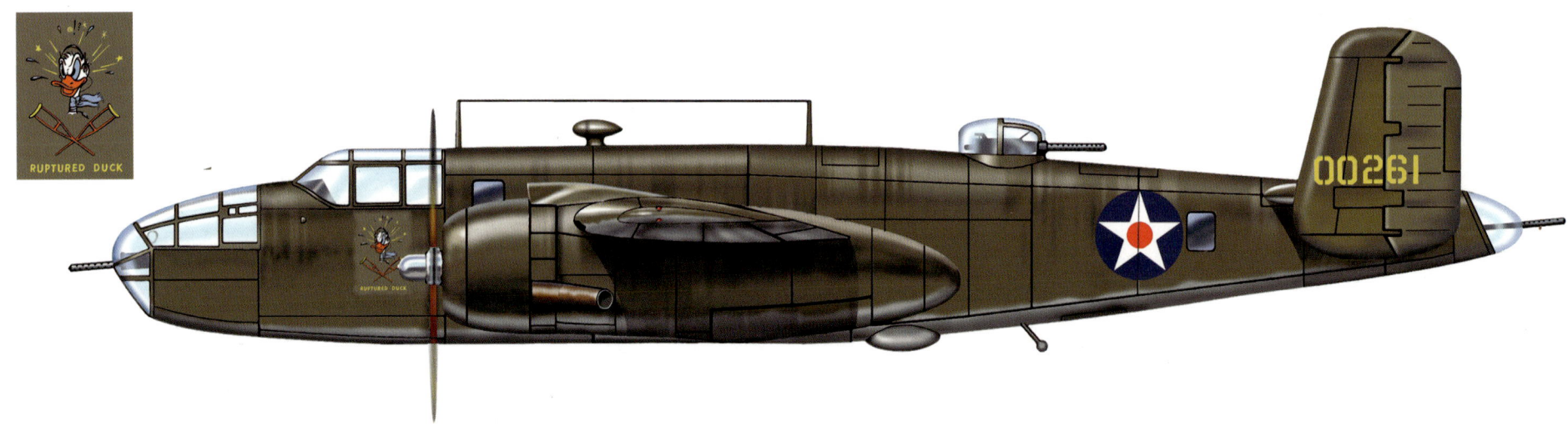

Lieutenant Colonel James "Jimmy" Doolittle, USAAF, left of center, commanded the Tokyo raid. The crewmen's leather flight jackets sport insignia of the 34th Bomb Squadron "Thunderbirds" and 37th Bomb Squadron "Lions." Next to Doolittle is Capt. Marc Mitscher, USN, commander of the *Hornet* and its task force. In the background is a B-25B with a cover over the engine. (National Museum of the United States Air Force)

Doolittle, second from left, poses with his personal crew from the 34th Bomb Squadron assigned to the number-one B-25B, serial number 40-2344, prior to the Tokyo raid (left to right): Lt. Henry A. Potter, navigator; Staff Sgt. Fred A. Braemer, bombardier; Lt. Richard E. Cole, copilot; and Staff Sgt. Paul J. Leonard, flight engineer/gunner. (National Museum of the United States Air Force)

Member's of Doolittle's USAAF crews load .50-caliber ammunition into magazines for the B25-B's top turrets on the flight deck of USS *Hornet* prior to the Tokyo raid, while navy crewmen look on. The man to the right of center is kneeling on a box of 200 rounds of mixed M2 armor-piercing, M1 incendiary, and M1 tracer ammunition. (National Museum of the United States Air Force)

A B-25B awaits the flag signal of the launch officer to the right, seconds before take off from the USS *Hornet* on 18 April 1942. The aircraft took off without the benefit of catapults, and conditions were marginal, with heavy seas, strong winds, and thick overcast. Doolittle's B-25B was the first into the air, at 0820. (National Museum of the United States Air Force)

19

One of Doolittle's B-25Bs has just cleared the flight deck of USS *Hornet*. All 16 of the bombers launched successfully. To dissuade Japanese interceptors from attacking the aircraft from the rear, two broomsticks, simulating machine guns, were inserted into the clear observation blister at the rear of each fuselage. (National Museum of the United States Air Force)

Following the Tokyo raid, plans were for the B-25Bs to land at friendly bases in China, but most of the crews had to crash-land or bail out in Japanese-held territory in China. Many sympathetic Chinese, including Tung-Sheng Liu (third from right, shown with the crew of Lt. Travis Hoover) helped the raiders escape. (National Museum of the United States Air Force)

The crews of two of Doolittle's B-25Bs were captured by the Japanese in occupied China. Lt. Robert Hite, shown being led from a transport plane by his captors, would spend 40 months as a P.O.W. Despite the loss of all of the aircraft and the sufferings of the crewmen, the Doolittle Raid was a resounding morale booster for the United States. (National Museum of the United States Air Force)

After Doolittle and his crew bailed out of their B-25B north of Quzhou ("Chuchow"), Zhejiang Province, China, the plane crashed on a mountaintop. Here, American airmen and friendly Chinese inspect the wreckage. Despite the marginal tactical success of the mission, Doolittle was promoted to brigadier general the day after the raid and went on to a distinguished Air Force career. (National Museum of the United States Air Force)

Armorers prepare bombs for a B-25B. In the early part of the U.S. involvement in World War II, high-explosive demolition and fragmentation bombs were painted yellow. Later, they would be painted matte olive drab. Visible on the tops of the bombs are the suspension lugs, by which the bombs were attached to the bomb racks. (Stan Piet collection)

The United States transferred hundreds of B-25s of different models to the British Royal Air Force during World War II. The RAF designated these bombers the Mitchell, Mks. I, II, and III. Pictured here is the first Mitchell I that the British acquired in the summer of 1942. The RAF gave this B-25B the aircraft number FK161.

The first RAF Mitchell I, FK161, was photographed during a test flight at the Aeroplane and Armament Experimental Establishment at Boscombe Down, Wiltshire, England. It was painted in a three-color camouflage scheme with sharp demarcation between the colors, and has an RAF roundel with a thin yellow border.

B-25C

The B-25C was the first model of the B-25 family to be produced in the thousands: 1,625 B-25Cs and its submodels would be built at North American's Inglewood, California, factory. Most of the B-25C's changes from the B-25B were internal, but one noticeable exterior modification was the blister-shaped tail skid that replaced the earlier skid. (Library of Congress)

To the roar of its R-2600-13 Wright Cyclone engines, the first B-25C lifted into the air from North American's Inglewood, California, facility on 9 November 1941. Deliveries to the Army began just after the first of the new year. During the interim, the Japanese attack on Pearl Harbor had brought the United States into World War II. Over the course of production, numerous minor improvements continued to be made to the B-25C. Armament, bomb racks, and exhaust stacks were among the areas improved during the production of the aircraft. Among the more significant changes were the following:

• Beginning with 41-12817, astrodomes began to replace the flat window on top of the navigator's compartment.

• External bomb racks under the wings and fuselage were added, starting with 41-13039. The under-fuselage rack could accommodate a 2,000-pound torpedo.

• The nose-mounted .30 caliber flexible machine gun was replaced with a more potent .50-caliber flexible gun at 42-53332. This change required strengthening the nose. A fixed, pilot-controlled .50-caliber gun was also added inside the nose, on the right side of the aircraft.

• At 42-32233, blisters replaced the navigator's flat side windows, and at 42-32383 individual flame-dampening stacks on each cylinder replaced the previously used single collector for each engine.

• Improved Bendix A-9 upper and A-10 lower turrets were installed starting with 42-64502. Nevertheless, almost 300 of the B-25D models were built without the lower gun turret due to production difficulties at Bendix.

• A redesigned windshield framework, introduced with 42-64702, improved the pilot's field of vision.

The Inglewood facility had turned out 1,625 of the B-25C model by May 1943, at which time production shifted to newer versions.

Technicians view a model of a B-25 during wind-tunnel tests in October 1942. Before any design was committed to production, the aerodynamic characteristics of the proposed aircraft had to be studied. An accurate scale model of the aircraft would be fashioned from composite materials and subjected to fan-generated air currents inside a wind tunnel. (Library of Congress)

A technician holds a model of an aerial torpedo below a B-25 model in a wind tunnel. The model features the belly turret in its lowered position. (Library of Congress)

A factory worker installs the ignition wiring harness on a Wright Cyclone engine. For the B-25C, the engines were upgraded to the Wright R-2600-13. (Library of Congress)

Wright Cyclone engines destined for installation on B-25s are lined up on a factory floor, complete with front cowl rings and cowl flaps. (Library of Congress)

A "Rosie the Riveter" assembles to the front of a B-25 fixed cowl one of the seven rubber-cushioned Lord mounts to which the engine-mounting frame was attached. (Library of Congress)

North American workers position an engine assembly for installation on the left nacelle of a B-25. Yellow zinc chromate primer covers skin surfaces. (Library of Congress)

Auxiliary, droppable fuel tanks that could be mounted in B-25 bomb bays are lined up at North American's Inglewood plant. Each tank held up to 418.8 U.S. gallons, appreciably extending the bomber's range during ferrying flights. (Library of Congress)

B-25Cs on the North American assembly line at Inglewood await installation of their outer wing panels. These bombers have a clear blister for the astro-compass on top of the fuselage behind the cockpit: a feature introduced with B-25C serial number 41-12817. North American assembled the B-25s in sections, making for faster, more efficient production. The center section of the fuselage also incorporated the inner wing sections, with the wing spars running through the fuselage above the bomb bay, resulting in a sturdy wing-to-fuselage joint. (Library of Congress)

Workers on the Inglewood sunshine assembly line apply paper masking to the glazing of the cockpit and the bombardier's compartment, preparatory to painting the aircraft. The frames of the clear enclosures have already been painted olive drab. (Library of Congress)

At the Inglewood plant, the outer wing sections have been installed on this B-25C, which has been painted overall in matte olive drab and neutral gray. Workers are putting the finishing touches on the aircraft. (Library of Congress)

An unpainted B-25C minus its outer wing panels is about to be moved outdoors to the North American Inglewood plant's "sunshine assembly line," where the bombers underwent further work under Southern California's usually fair skies. (Library of Congress)

Nearly finished B-25Cs on the tarmac at North American's Inglewood, California, plant await delivery to the U.S. Army Air Forces. Mooring lines are affixed to the wings and fuselages to prevent the wind from moving and damaging the bombers. (Library of Congress)

Several Mitchell medium bombers, evidently B-25Cs, sit on a tarmac. The clear blister at the rear of the fuselage provided a vantage point for observing the effects of a bombing run. Details of the rudder and trim tab are visible. (National Archives)

An International tractor is hitched up to the front landing gear of a B-25C at Inglewood to tow the bomber off the sunshine assembly line. A worker is sitting at the pilot's controls in the cockpit, presumably to operate the brakes as necessary. (Library of Congress)

A security guard stands watch among a group of completed B-25Cs at North American Aviation's Inglewood factory. The ball sockets for machine guns in the front and the left side of the bombardier's clear enclosure are visible. Black deicer panels are on the leading edges of the wings. (Library of Congress)

Waist machine guns were restored on some B-25Cs, with the work being performed in the field or at various modification centers. Cutouts allow the barrel of this .50-caliber machine gun to protrude even when this right-side sliding window is closed.

Dis'n Did't, a B-25-C-1, serial number 41-13084, served with the 310th Bomb Group, 381st Bomb Squadron, in the Mediterranean. The main changes of the B-25C1 from the B-25C were the addition of under-wing bomb racks, strengthened outer wing sections, and provisions for a torpedo rack. (Stan Piet collection)

B-25C s/n 41-12971 served in the 405th Bomb Squadron and then the 71st Bomb Squadron before gunship conversion at the modification center at Townsville, Australia, in July 1943. She was sent to the 345th Bomb Group, 499th Bomb Squadron, in New Guinea where Lt. Vic Tatelman, the new pilot, renamed her *Dirty Dora*. (Stan Piet collection)

Miss Nashville, s/n 42-53357, was one of only two 8th Air Force B-25s in the UK. Painted in overall-black night camouflage in August 1944, this B-26C flew 13 nocturnal photo missions over V-1 installations with the 7th Photo Group. (Robert Astrella)

28

A tractor prepares to tow a B-25C. The bulged side windows in the navigator's compartment were introduced with that model. The socket mounts for a .30-caliber machine gun in the sides of the bombardier's clear enclosure were eventually discontinued in later C-series B-25s. (Stan Piet collection)

This B-25C wears a camouflage scheme designed for service in North Africa: sand on the upper and side surfaces and neutral gray on the lower surfaces. It exhibits the bulged side windows and clear blister in the navigator's compartment and machine gun sockets on the bombardier compartment's side windows. (USAF)

The tail number 112856 is painted in matte yellow on the first bomber in a row of B-25Cs wearing the "sand and neutral gray" camouflage colors. The tail number was equivalent to the serial number with the first digit omitted. In the serial number of this aircraft, 41-12856, the 41 stands for the year of the contract for this model, 1941. (USAF)

From what is visible of the tail number of this bomber, 2325 (the last two digits are illegible), this is a B-25C-15. This submodel introduced Clayton S-type flame-dampening exhausts on each engine cylinder, with small fairings on the cowling over each exhaust, instead of a single exhaust stack on the side of each nacelle. (National Archives)

A flight of Mitchells of the Twelfth Air Force cruises off the coast of North Africa. The bombers are painted in sand and neutral gray, with red, white, and blue recognition flashes and white aircraft numbers on the vertical stabilizers. The national insignia are surrounded by the wide yellow border used for Operation Torch. (Stan Piet collection)

A B-25C, serial number 41-12863, of the 12th Bomb Group, 82nd Bomb Squadron, skims above the Western Desert, accompanied by several other Mitchells. Atop the fuselage to the front of the ADF antenna is the astrodome introduced with B-25C serial number 41-12817. The individual aircraft number, 33, is painted on the vertical tail. (National Archives)

B-25Cs of the 12th Bomb Group, 82nd Bomb Squadron, fly a combat mission against Axis targets in Tunisia in January 1943. In the background are several RAF Martin Baltimore bombers that are cooperating in the mission. The small fairings over the two right oil cooler outlets on the B-25C's wing were not repeated on the left wing. (National Archives)

Crewmembers of *Oh-7* prepare to take off on a mission over North Africa. This bomber was B-25C serial number 41-13207, assigned to the 321st Bomb Group, 445th Bomb Squadron, of the Twelfth Air Force. The bomber flew more than 80 combat missions in North Africa and Italy from March 1943 to January 1944. (Stan Piet collection)

Desert Warrior, B-25C serial number 41-12480, flew 73 missions with the 12th Bomb Group, 81st Bomb Squadron, from Harqalah ("Hergla"), Tunisia, before being returned to the United States on a war-bond drive, complete with special nose art for the occasion, including a map of the bomber's missions. (National Archives)

A Chevrolet 1½-ton bomb service truck pulls a U.S. M5 bomb trailer past the same Mitchell as in the previous photograph (above right). The bomb service truck features a hoist for loading and unloading bombs from the trailer. In the background is a British bomb trailer with a different configuration of wheels. (National Archives)

A maintenance crew readies a B-25 for a mission in late 1942. The aircraft already shows wear and tear from hard service, including heavily worn paint and a badly bent cowl flap. B-25s in North Africa often worked out of primitive, dusty air fields. (National Archives)

Seen from the left, the same aircraft appears to be a B-25C or C-1 with some C-5 - type modifications, including the elimination of the side machine gun sockets in the clear nose, the addition of a fixed .50-caliber machine gun in the right side of the nose, and a metal plate to hold the socket of the flex .50-caliber machine gun in the nose. (National Archives)

At a Twelfth Air Force airfield, a cluster of fragmentation bombs (lower right) is about to be hoisted into the bomb bay of a Mitchell prior to an air raid mission in support of Allied troops on the beachheads south of Rome. To the left side are more clusters of bombs, while in the background is a fuel truck. (National Archives)

Armorers roll 1,000-pound bombs over Marston matting to a Mitchell medium bomber of the Twelfth Air Force. This plane is apparently a B-25C-5 or C-10 (or possibly a B-25D-1 to D-10), judging from the absence of a single exhaust on the side of the nacelle. Modified waist gun mounts have been installed. (National Archives)

321st Bomb Group armorers position a 1,000-pound bomb below the bomb bay of a Mitchell medium bomber. The tail fin and fuses will be installed after the bomb is on its rack. The inner lining of the bomb bay doors were perforated with lightening holes. Aft of the bomb bay is the rear crew door with collapsible ladder. (National Archives)

Staff Sergeant Jack A. Fleethe, right, uses a hand-operated Type C bomb hoist attached to the side of the fuselage to lift a 1,000-bomb up to its bomb rack. Steadying the bomb are, left to right, Staff Sgt. Roy T. Peterson and Tech Sgt. Ervin T. Dickey. The scene was a Twelfth Air Force base in Italy. (National Archives)

A B-25C-1, serial number 41-013070, based with the 310th Bomb Group, Twelfth Air Force at Berteaux, near Talâghmah, Algeria, flies a mission against an Axis target. Although the B-25C-5 was reportedly the first submodel of the Mitchell to have finger-type flame-dampening exhausts, this type of exhausts is visible on this aircraft. (National Archives)

An armorer steadies a bomb in a sling as it is hoisted in the bomb bay of a Mitchell medium bomber during Operation Strangle, an air campaign intended to break up German lines of transportation north of Rome between 1943 and 1944. His right hand is resting on a bomb shackle attached to the bomb. (National Archives)

A Mitchell medium bomber flies at low level over the North African desert *en route* to an enemy target. Shadows of other B-25s in the formation are cast on the ground. Black deicer boots are visible on the leading edges of the wings, horizontal stabilizers, and vertical stabilizers. (National Archives)

Two Mitchells speed across the desert. From what is visible of the serial number of the closer bomber, it is a B-25C or B-25C-1. The other bomber, evidently a B-25C, has been upgraded with individual exhausts on each engine cylinder, with corresponding fairings on the cowl. (National Archives)

Staff Sergeant Billy Dykes of the 321st Bomb Group, 446th Bomb Squadron, poses beside his top turret, which was shattered by enemy flak during a raid on Gerbini, Sicily, on 5 July 1943. The flak took away most of the clear Plexiglas enclosure of the turret and left Dykes with several wounds. (National Archives)

This close-up shows another top turret that suffered severe damage. This turret on a Twelfth Air Force B-25 based at Berteaux, Algeria, was savaged by a Messerschmitt Bf 109 on 7 March 1943, shattering the Plexiglas enclosure, puncturing the gun sight, and putting out one of the gunner's eyes. (National Archives)

A Sikh stands guard over a B-25 of the 341st Bomb Group in India. The bomber is of one of the -C or -D submodels of the B-25 and exhibits a fixed machine gun in the nose. On the cowl are the fairings for the individual Clayton S-type flame-dampening exhausts that became factory standard with the B-25C-15. (National Archives)

A B-25 of the -C or -D series assigned to the 341st Bomb Group in India is undergoing refueling. The socket for a machine gun in the side of the bombardier's clear enclosure is an early -C and -D series feature, while the Clayton exhausts are characteristic of later aircraft, thus this aircraft has been modified. (National Archives)

Armorers of the 341st Bomb Group in India roll bombs from an M5 bomb trailer to a B-25. Four fixed machine guns protrude from the clear nose of this aircraft. The aircraft's call numbers, 00, are painted in black toward the front of the fuselage and in white on the front wheel hub cap. (National Archives)

A group of officers poses next to a weather-beaten B-25 named *Roger the Lodger* at India-China Wing ATC Station #4 Jorhat, India Station. The 92 bombs painted on the fuselage signify bombing missions, and two other symbols stand for ships destroyed. (National Museum of the United States Air Force)

PBJ-1C

Recognizing the adaptability of the B-25 to anti-shipping and anti-submarine operations, the U.S. Navy procured a number of the bombers. But by the time the B-25s were ready for delivery in early 1943, the Navy no longer had a need for them, having in the meantime acquired the more potent PB4Y-1 and PV-1. Nonetheless, the Navy saw a role for the B-25 in U.S. Marine Corps aviation operations and embarked on a procurement program for the USMC, redesignating the B-25B the PBJ-1 (J was the USN code for North American Aviation). Subsequent PBJ-1s received letter suffixes of C, D, G, H, and J, corresponding to the B-25C through the B-25J. The Marines obtained a total of 706 of these bombers, which were distributed to an operational training squadron and 16 bomb squadrons. This example is reportedly a PBJ-1C. (Air Force Historical Research Agency)

The PBJ-1C and PBJ-1D were outwardly similar, the C model being produced at the Inglewood plant and the D model being made at North American Aviation's Kansas City, Kansas, facility. Fairings for the Clayton S-type exhausts are arrayed around the cowl, and deicer boots are installed on the wings and horizontal and vertical stabilizers.

Although the Navy originally envisioned the Marines' using the PBJ-1 for anti-submarine and coastal patrols, the Leathernecks also adapted it to ground-attack operations in the island-hopping campaigns in the Pacific Ocean. The many later additions to the basic PBJ-1C seen here would include gun packs, rockets, and radar.

PBJ-1 (B-25D) of the U.S. Marine Corps operates near Espirito Santo, in the New Hebrides Island group during February of 1944. The aircraft is camouflaged in blue-gray over light gray. A field-modified tail gunner's position has been added and .50 caliber guns protrude from the waist hatches.

B-25D

When the demand for B-25s exceeded North American's ability to produce them at its Inglewood, California, plant, the company set up a second assembly line at its factory in Kansas City, Kansas. The first type of B-25 produced there was the B-25D, which was essentially identical to the B-25C. B-25Ds are shown in construction in October 1942. On the aircraft in the foreground, the empennage (rear vertical and horizontal tail unit) is being lowered into place. Unlike the more complete aircraft seen in the background, the airframes in the foreground still lack their outer wing sections. (Library of Congress)

Following the US entry into the war, orders for arms, including the Mitchell, increased dramatically. In fact, North American's Inglewood facility had inadequate capacity to meet the demand for the Mitchell and its stable mate, the P-51 Mustang. Two solutions to this problem were employed. First, final assembly work was moved to an out-of-doors production line. Secondly, an additional manufacturing center was established in Kansas City, Kansas.

While B-25C production continued in California, essentially identical aircraft built in the Midwest plant were designated B-25D. Production of the B-25D began in the latter half of 1942, with the first B-25D being delivered two days before Christmas of that year. While the last B-25C rolled out of Inglewood in May 1943, production of the B-25D continued until March 1944. There were thus two more production blocks of the latter, with additional improvements made in each.

The Kansas City facility was essentially an assembly plant. While the components for the first 100 B-25Ds were produced by North American at Inglewood and shipped to Kansas City, the balance of the KC production was done with General Motors's Fisher Body Division supplying the bulk of the components from its plants in Memphis, Tennessee, and Cleveland, Ohio. North American Aviation in Inglewood supplied specialized machine parts. While the initial plan called for Fisher to supply 55% of the value of the aircraft, with North American's assembly accounting for 45%, the Kansas City plant gradually expanded into manufacturing as well, until ultimately Kansas City was imparting 71% of the aircraft's value.

Big Time Operator **was a B-25D-10 serial number 41-30188, stationed in New Guinea in 1943. The bomber was painted overall in matte black as a camouflage measure for night operations. It bears markings representing 26 bombing missions, and the three small Japanese flags represent three enemy aircraft claimed as killed. (Stan Piet collection)**

The outer wing sections have been mounted on this B-25D at the Kansas City plant. Masking paper has been applied to some of the clear panels of the bombardier's compartment. Some of the skin panels are still bare aluminum, while others have been given a coat of yellow primer. Deicers are installed on the leading edges of the wings. (USAF)

Chow Hound Junior, a B-25D, is attached to the 499th Bomb Squadron of the 345th Bomb Group "Air Apaches" in the Pacific. The aircraft is in a bare-aluminum finish with a matte antiglare panel (probably olive drab) to the front of the cockpit windshield, and stripes of indistinct colors on the tips of the propellers. (Stan Piet collection)

The nose art of *Chow Hound Junior* is shown in closer detail. The symbol of the Air Apaches, an Indian chief's head inside a circle, prominently displayed on the vertical tails, is repeated in smaller format on the picnic basket. There are blanked-over panels on both sides of the bombardier's clear enclosure. (Stan Piet collection)

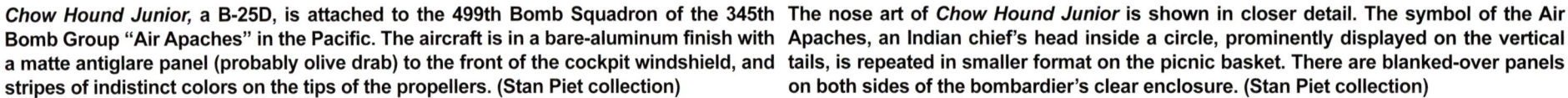

Pacific Prowler, B-25D serial number 41-29710, served with the 38th Bomb Group in New Guinea. The name of the pilot, Capt. Bill Tarver, is written below the cockpit canopy, while the names of the bombardier, Jim Craig, and the navigator, Ed Gervase, are stenciled in white below their respective side windows. (National Museum of the United States Air Force)

Pacific Prowler was also photographed from below. A metal-reinforced machine-gun socket mount was installed below the blanked-over original opening for the socket on the side of the bombardier's canopy. Below bombardier Craig's name is written, "Jeanne — Queen of the Bluegrass." On the left engine nacelle is written the word "Repeat." (National Museum of the United States Air Force)

This view of a late B-25C or B-25D does not depict a real plane named *Spirit of Edgewater B'nai B'rith*. Rather, it was a skillful photo-manipulation whereby the serial number was removed and the aircraft name was overprinted in a cynical ploy to "prove" that funds raised by this Chicago Jewish group had helped build a particular bomber. (National Museum of the United States Air Force)

Dirty Gerty from Binzart ("*Bizerte*"), Tunisia, was named after a soldiers' song of World War II. She was a B-25D-1, serial number 41-29896, reportedly assigned to the 3rd Attack Group in Australia in 1942. The aircraft exhibits many splotches of dark paint, possibly to touch-up damaged or repaired skin and to seal joints in the skin. (National Museum of the United States Air Force)

The flight crew and ground crew of *The "Nip" Clipper*, a B-25D, stand before their bomber. The serial number of the aircraft to the left identifies it as a B-25C that at one time was with the 312th Bomb Group, 398th Bomb Squadron. The first and third crewmen from the left appear to be wearing Australian uniforms. (National Museum of the United States Air Force)

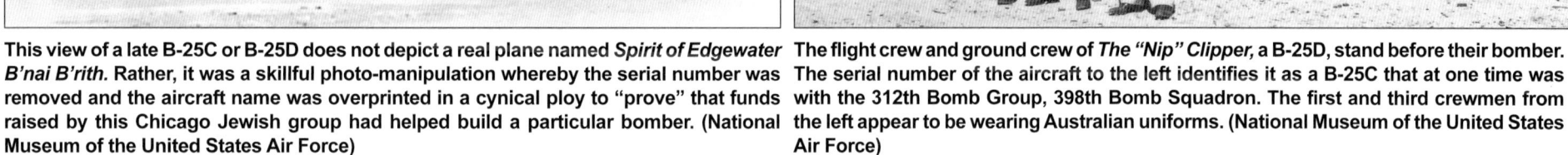

This B-25D, serial number 41-29738, was nicknamed *Iroquois* and served with the 3rd Attack Group based in Australia in 1942. The small diagonal tube projecting from the bottom of the fuselage to the rear of the bottom turret was the nozzle for the trailing antenna, a wire radio antenna that was fed out to trail behind the aircraft when needed. (National Museum of the United States Air Force)

Bomb-bay doors open, a Mitchell medium bomber circles in for the attack on a Japanese ship in Hansa Bay on the north coast of New Guinea. The tail number is indistinct but appears to be 130434, which would make this a B-25D-15. Three circular ripples from bomb strikes are visible around the sailing ship. (National Museum of the United States Air Force)

Pannell Job, a B-25D-5 serial number 41-30024 of the 345th Bomb Group, 500th Bomb Squadron "Rough Raiders," flies a bombing mission over Wakde Island, off the northern coast of New Guinea, on 11 May 1944. The aircraft was named after the pilot, Lt. Ray Pannell. The tail sports the snorting mustang insignia of the 500th Bomb Squadron. (National Museum of the United States Air Force)

On 22 March 1944, Mt. Vesuvius erupted, spewing hot volcanic ash that burned the control surfaces off of the B-25Cs and B-25Ds of the 340th Bomb Group, stationed near Pompeii. The ash also etched the exposed Plexiglas glazing everywhere on the aircraft.

A veteran of over 190 missions, *Mitch the Witch* was B-25D-25 serial number 42-87293, first assigned to the 38th Bomb Group and later transferred to the 71st Tactical Recon Group, 17th Tactical Recon Squadron. The bottom part of the clear Plexiglas nose is painted over. The witch's broom features vertical B-25 tails. (Stan Piet collection)

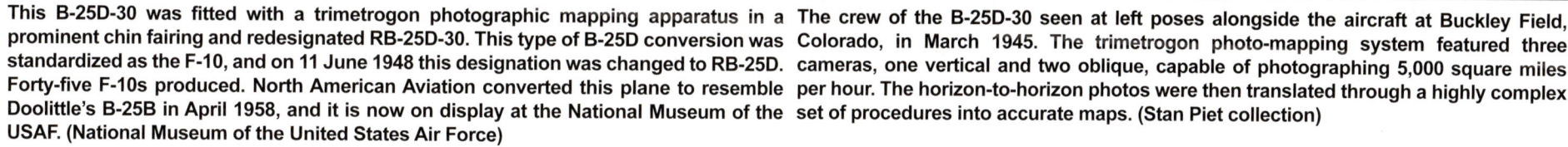

This B-25D-30 was fitted with a trimetrogon photographic mapping apparatus in a prominent chin fairing and redesignated RB-25D-30. This type of B-25D conversion was standardized as the F-10, and on 11 June 1948 this designation was changed to RB-25D. Forty-five F-10s produced. North American Aviation converted this plane to resemble Doolittle's B-25B in April 1958, and it is now on display at the National Museum of the USAF. (National Museum of the United States Air Force)

The crew of the B-25D-30 seen at left poses alongside the aircraft at Buckley Field, Colorado, in March 1945. The trimetrogon photo-mapping system featured three cameras, one vertical and two oblique, capable of photographing 5,000 square miles per hour. The horizon-to-horizon photos were then translated through a highly complex set of procedures into accurate maps. (Stan Piet collection)

A B-25D-1, serial number 41-29899, of the India-China Wing, Air Transport Command, flies a search mission over Burma, seeking downed Allied aircraft or aircrews. The paint on the aircraft exhibits extensive discoloration from prolonged service in the heat and humidity of Southeast Asia. (National Archives)

Lady Jane, B-25D-15 serial number 41-30409, served with the 26th Antisubmarine Wing, 23rd Antisubmarine Squadron. Based in Florida, the squadron transitioned to B-25s at Langley Field, Virginia, in July 1943. The bomber has the so-called "Sea-Search" camouflage scheme, most likely the spring 1943 version, with olive drab over white. (National Museum of the United States Air Force)

The PBJ-1D was the Navy version of the B-25D. This particular example served as a flight-test and evaluation aircraft at NAS Patuxent River, Maryland, where it was photographed on 31 May 1944. On the side of the fuselage below the cockpit is a gun pack containing two .50-caliber M2 machine guns. (National Museum of Naval Aviation)

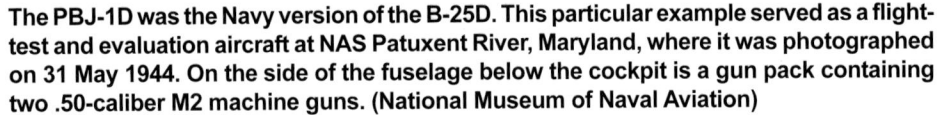

A PBJ-1D marked with the code "R109" and assigned to an unidentified training squadron flies with an escort of two Corsair fighters over the desert near Marine Corps Air Station El Centro, California. Two T-shaped radio altimeter antennas are mounted on the underside of the fuselage aft of the wings. (National Museum of Naval Aviation)

Marine PBJ-1 aircraft of the -C or -D submodels are being ferried on the flight deck of the escort carrier USS *Kalinin Bay* (CVE-68), seen here entering Pearl Harbor during her first combat cruise. Specially fitted waterproof covers protect the turrets, cockpit canopies, astrodomes, engines, and propellers of the aircraft. (National Museum of Naval Aviation)

Marine PBJ-1Ds of VMB-413 fly South Pacific skies in late March 1944. These aircraft are fitted with .50-caliber machine gun packs on the fuselage below the cockpit as well as radomes for the S-band search radar in the location formerly occupied by the bottom turret. The radar sets were the AN/APS-2 or AN/APS-3. (National Museum of Naval Aviation)

Bearing the black number 43, the PBJ-1D of VMB-413 seen in the bottom-right photo on the preceding page is shown here in closer detail. Aft of the radome on the bottom of the fuselage are two T-shaped radio altimeter antennas. In addition to the socket-mounted .50-caliber machine gun in the front of the clear nose, there are two fixed .50s on the right side of the nose. (National Museum of Naval Aviation)

Mechanics service a Mitchell of Marine Air Wing 4 at Motoyama Air Field, Iwo Jima, prior to embarking on an anti-shipping mission in 1945. Under the wing of this aircraft, a PBJ-1D (or possibly -C), are zero-length launchers for 5-inch HVAR air-to-surface rockets. Cowl panels with individual exhaust fairings are on the ground. (National Archives)

A PBJ-1D, probably with VMB-413, drops bombs on a Japanese target in March 1944. This bomber is one of those fitted with a tail gun installation mounting a single .50-caliber machine gun. This gun installation appears to have been the type installed on some B-25s and PBJs by the Hawaiian Air Depot. It featured a raised canopy with a flat rear aiming window. (National Museum of Naval Aviation)

Forty-two members of the Philadelphia South Pacific Club pose in front of a PBJ-1C or -D at an advanced air base. This club, consisting of more than 50 members, represented the largest circle of men all hailing from one city in the unidentified air group. (National Archives)

An RAF Mitchell Mk. II, aircraft number FV916 and squadron/aircraft code EV-N of No. 180 Squadron, is being refueled at Dunsford, Surrey, in support of Operation Starkey, an Allied feint at a cross-Channel invasion, 9 September 1943. Mitchells Mk. II were predominantly based on the B-25C and B-25D; this Mitchell Mk. II was based on the D.

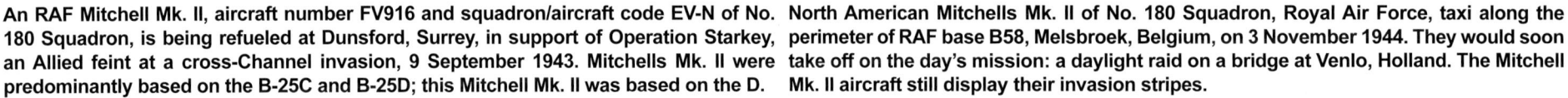

Preparing for a mission on 8 January 1945, ground crewmen sweep fresh snow from a Mitchell Mk. II of No. 320 (Dutch) Squadron at RAF Airfield B58, Melsbroek, Belgium. This squadron, composed of expatriate members of the Royal Netherlands Naval Air Service, had been flying the Mitchell Mk. II since March 1943.

North American Mitchells Mk. II of No. 180 Squadron, Royal Air Force, taxi along the perimeter of RAF base B58, Melsbroek, Belgium, on 3 November 1944. They would soon take off on the day's mission: a daylight raid on a bridge at Venlo, Holland. The Mitchell Mk. II aircraft still display their invasion stripes.

North American Mitchells Mk. II of No. 98 Squadron, RAF, taxi to the runway at Dunsfold, Surrey, on 21 April 1944. The day's mission was a morning raid on targets in northern France. The individual letter of the lead aircraft, D, is painted on the fuselage to the front of the wing. The nose gun is equipped with a conical flash suppressor.

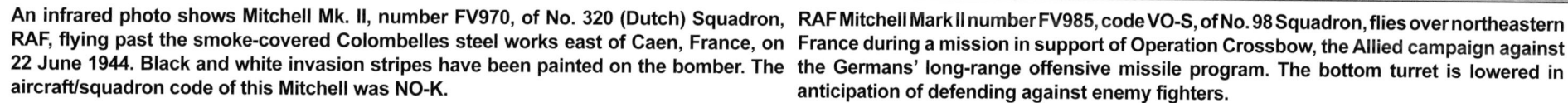

An infrared photo shows Mitchell Mk. II, number FV970, of No. 320 (Dutch) Squadron, RAF, flying past the smoke-covered Colombelles steel works east of Caen, France, on 22 June 1944. Black and white invasion stripes have been painted on the bomber. The aircraft/squadron code of this Mitchell was NO-K.

On the last day of 1944, RAF and Dutch ground crewmen prepare to load 500-pound MC bombs into Mitchells Mk. II of No. 98 Squadron, RAF, at airfield B58, Melsbroek, Belgium. Like the USAAF bomb trailers, the RAF bomb trailers could be hitched in trains, but the RAF trailers had smaller wheels and lower ground clearance.

RAF Mitchell Mark II number FV985, code VO-S, of No. 98 Squadron, flies over northeastern France during a mission in support of Operation Crossbow, the Allied campaign against the Germans' long-range offensive missile program. The bottom turret is lowered in anticipation of defending against enemy fighters.

A Mitchell Mark II, number FV914 and code VO-A, of No. 98 Squadron, RAF, drops its payload of bombs on a German missile launch site in northern France as part of Operation Crossbow. The bomber was photographed from the left waist window of another Mitchell in the formation. A vertical stabilizer is visible to the left.

B-25G

The early Mitchell medium bombers had proven themselves well suited to ground-attack and surface-shipping-attack roles when modified with extra fixed guns. The B-25G program was intended to standardize a Mitchell gunship. Using a B-25C-1 as the basis for a prototype XB-25G, a snubbed nose section was substituted for the bombardier's compartment. Two .50-caliber machine guns and their magazines were mounted in this nose, and an M4 75mm cannon was installed in the crawlway located below the left side of the cockpit. Including the B-25G prototype, 405 aircraft were produced in this series at North American's Inglewood plant, including the B-25G-1, B-25G-5, and B-25G-10. The aircraft in this photo is a very late B-25G-10. (Air Force Historical Research Agency)

One each of the experimental XB-25E and XB-25F were converted from production B-25C aircraft in order to test various methods of wing deicing. Neither of these variants ever saw production. A third B-25C, 41-13296, was also modified to X-plane status, becoming the XB-25G. The "greenhouse" nose was replaced with a shorter, metal nose. Housed within the nose, near the vertical centerline of the fuselage, were two .50-caliber machine guns mounted abreast. Beneath them, extending back into the area formerly used as the bombardier's crawlway, was the B-25G's Sunday punch, a 75mm cannon.

The M-4, and later M-6, 75mm cannon was essentially a tank gun firing an 18-pound round. Fired by the pilot, the gun was hand-loaded by the navigator. Twenty-one rounds was the normal ammunition load for the big gun, while each of the twin nose-mounted .50-calibers had its own 400-round magazine. Devastating in its own right, the gunfire of the machine guns also helped the pilot aim the cannon.

First flown in October 1942, the XB-25G was extensively tested. In January 1943, five more B-25C aircraft, 42-32384 through 42-32388, were converted to G status for additional service testing.

North American's contract for B-25C aircraft was modified, specifying that 400 of the bombers were to be completed in B-25G configuration. This task was accomplished from May to August 1943. A further 63 previously built B-25Cs were converted to B-25G standards.

A little more than half of new B-25G models (42-64802 – 42-65201) were equipped with the ventral power turret, before it was eliminated, beginning with 42-65102.

In part resultant from the elimination of this turret, many of the B-25Gs had tail positions with single .50-caliber machine guns added at modification centers. Waist gun positions were sometimes added as well.

One of the distinguishing characteristics of this aircraft is the sheet metal shield obscuring the lower left side of the windscreen. This shield was intended to prevent the cannon's muzzle flash from blinding or distracting the pilot.

The U.S. Navy received one of these aircraft, which it designated PBJ-1G.

The B-25G prototype still wears its original B-25C-1 tail number, 113296 (a new number, 43-32372, would be assigned to this prototype). The 75mm gun alone weighed 893 pounds, and up to 21 rounds of 75mm ammunition, each weighing about 18 pounds, could be carried in a rack. Each .50-caliber nose gun had 400 rounds of ammunition. (National Museum of the United States Air Force)

The M4 75mm cannon rested on an M6 recoil mount. Only the front several inches of the gun barrel protruded through a recess in the nose. The navigator loaded the piece one round at a time. The .50-caliber machine guns, shown here with protective wrappings, could be used as spotting weapons to align the big gun on target. (National Museum of the United States Air Force)

A B-25G-10 is photographed during a shakedown flight. The lower turret (not seen in this photo) had been eliminated partway through the B-25G-5 production run and would not be seen in future Mitchell medium bombers. This left only the top turret for defensive fire, although some B-25Gs had tail turrets installed as a modification. (National Museum of the United States Air Force)

In addition to the 405 aircraft bearing designations between B-25G and B-25G-10, North American's Kansas City Modification Center converted a total of 63 B-25Cs, B-25C-20s, and B-25C-25s to B-25G standards. This example, seen with its bottom turret retracted, still wears a tail number reflecting its B-25C-25 serial number, 42-64758. (National Archives)

This aircraft is the second B-25G-5 produced. It is still fitted with the bottom turret, shown here retracted. The metal panel that fills up the bottom half of the windshield panel to the pilot's left front was a standardized feature intended to shield the pilot's eyes from the flash of the 75mm gun. This feature carried over to subsequent models of the B-25. (National Museum of the United States Air Force)

A B-25G, probably the same one seen in the photograph at left, conducts tests from the USAAF Technical Center at Orlando, Florida. The national star under the right wing appears to have been painted over a large circle of touch-up paint, and the bars on each side of that insignia are blue outlines only, without the white centers painted in. (National Museum of the United States Air Force)

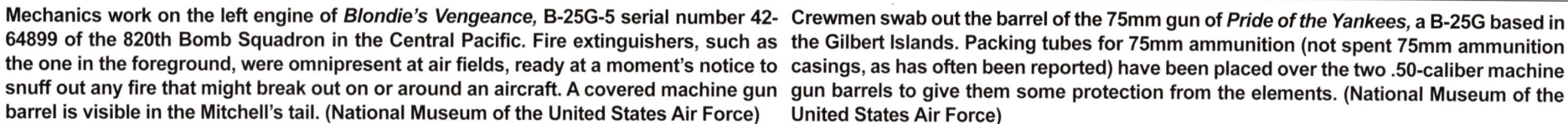

Mechanics work on the left engine of *Blondie's Vengeance,* B-25G-5 serial number 42-64899 of the 820th Bomb Squadron in the Central Pacific. Fire extinguishers, such as the one in the foreground, were omnipresent at air fields, ready at a moment's notice to snuff out any fire that might break out on or around an aircraft. A covered machine gun barrel is visible in the Mitchell's tail. (National Museum of the United States Air Force)

Crewmen swab out the barrel of the 75mm gun of *Pride of the Yankees,* a B-25G based in the Gilbert Islands. Packing tubes for 75mm ammunition (not spent 75mm ammunition casings, as has often been reported) have been placed over the two .50-caliber machine gun barrels to give them some protection from the elements. (National Museum of the United States Air Force)

The tiger-head artwork on the nose of this B-25G was a trademark of the 823rd Bomb Squadron "Terrible Tigers" of the 38th Bomb Group, Fifth Air Force. The aircraft was probably photographed at Nadzab, New Guinea, in 1944. The front cowl rings and the bottom parts of the vertical tails of this squadron's bombers were reportedly painted blue. (National Museum of the United States Air Force)

Two Mitchells, including a B-25G, bank over a coastal landscape. The faint horizontal line above the two .50-caliber machine guns on the nose represents the bottom edge of a hinged hood. Opening the hood provided access to the machine guns, the flex chutes for their ammunition, the ammunition magazines, and other components in the nose. (Stan Piet collection)

This B-25G has suffered a ground accident, and all propeller blades are bent, indicating the engine was still running when the aircraft hit the ground. The slightly dark panel on the side of the fuselage below the pilot's side windows is a ⅜-inch appliqué armor plate, a feature introduced to the Mitchells with the B-25G series. (Stan Piet collection)

These two Mitchells, including a B-25G in the foreground, are seen on the set of the 1945 movie, *God Is My Co-pilot,* most likely at some location in Southern California. The hood of the nose machine gun compartment is raised, revealing that the magazines for the two .50-caliber machine guns were not installed.

This B-25G gunship of the 499th BS, 345th BG, operates from Biak Island off northwest New Guinea in 1944. The U.S. insignia still lacks the blue outline. The cowl rings are blue and the starboard cowl ring has a thin white outline. The 75mm nose gun has been replaced by two machine guns. The ventral turret has been deleted and waist guns added.

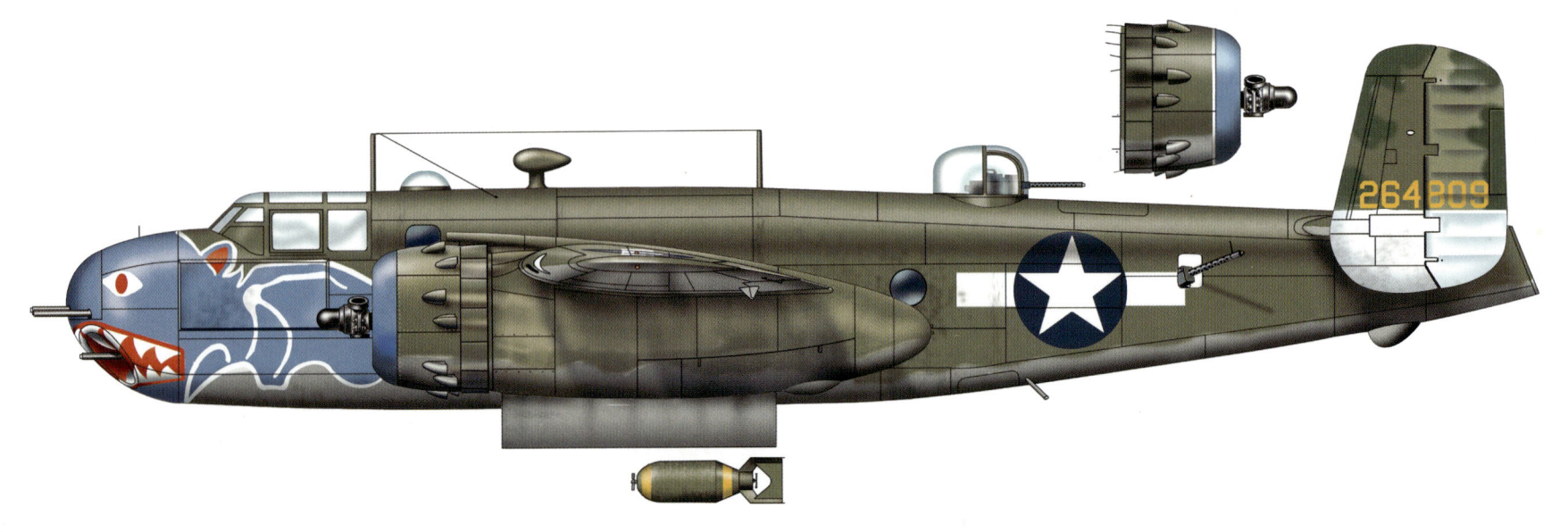

B-25H

The B-25H was an improved version of the 75mm gunship concept pioneered by the B-25G. It retained the same snubbed-nose shape, but four .50-caliber machine guns were installed in it instead of two. A lighter 75mm gun, the T13, was substituted for the M4 type and was installed on the T13E1 cannon mount. The copilot was eliminated from the crew; his controls and seat were removed, and a jump seat was installed for the relocated navigator, who doubled as cannoneer. To improve the aircraft's center of gravity, the top turret was moved forward to behind the cockpit. Moving the turret opened up the aft compartment for defensive waist guns, so bowed windows for machine guns were installed. Also, the rear fuselage was deepened in order to allow the addition of a new Bell M7 electro-hydraulic tail turret. (Air Force Historical Research Agency)

This B-25H-1 is part of the first production block of 300 aircraft following the B-25H prototype. Moving the turret forward necessitated deleting the astrodome and relocating the ADF antenna, which was repositioned on the bottom of the fuselage below the cockpit. The electrically operated Bendix top turret was controlled by an amplidyne. Each gun had a 400-round magazine. (Air Force Historical Research Agency)

Although the B-25G satisfied strategists' requirements for a heavy-hitting aircraft capable of shipping interdiction and attack on ground targets, its self-defense capabilities were somewhat limited. Accordingly, B-25C 42-32372 was selected as a test bed for further improvements. The result of these experiments, the B-25H, not only rectified the defensive problem, but increased the aircraft's assault firepower as well.

Moving the dorsal turret forward into the navigator's compartment freed space in the aft fuselage for installation of staggered waist-gun positions, each armed with a .50-caliber machine gun. The tail, which had been without a factory-installed gun position since the B-25A, was deepened and a Bell-designed M7 electro-hydraulic twin .50-caliber tail gun installation was fitted. The gunner sat beneath a greenhouse-type canopy at the bomber's rear, which was slightly wider than it had been on previous models.

A notable change on the flight deck was the elimination of the copilot, his position and controls. The instrument panel was redesigned to accommodate a single pilot better, and sights were added for both bombardment and cannon fire. Armor plate was installed outside the cockpit for additional protection.

An improved, lighter, T13E1 cannon was installed, once again being manually loaded by the navigator. In the solid nose, the two machine guns of the B-25G were doubled, with four of the heavy weapons being mounted abreast. Occasional shortages of the T13E1 weapon sometimes forced the installation of the older M-4, which in turn required the elimination of the two outer nose machine guns.

Even more strafing power was added, initially by the addition of two individually mounted .50-caliber gun packs on the right side of the fuselage beneath the cockpit. Then, after 300 aircraft were produced in this configuration, two gun packs began to be installed on the left side as well, in an arrangement that was retained on the remaining 700 B-25H models built.

The pilot's flash shield was carried over from the B-25G. A circular escape hatch was added to the right rear side of the fuselage, and the air intakes at the top of the nacelles were enlarged. After 43-4535, the B-25H could no longer carry a 2,000-pound bomb.

Production spanned from August 1943 into July 1944. Given North American Aviation model number NA-98, the B-25H aircraft were assigned these Army Air Force serial numbers: B-24H-1, 43-4105-4404; B-25H-5, 43-4405-4704; and B-25H-10, 43-4705-5104. *Old Bones,* the final B-25H, was also the last Mitchell built in California.

For use by the Marines, 236 of the B-25Hs were acquired by the Navy and given the Naval designation of PBJ-1H. These aircraft were pulled from lots ordered by the Army, and therefore on paper were originally assigned Army serial numbers, even though they left the factory wearing Navy colors, and bearing Bureau of Ships numbers. The Army serial numbers were not sequential. The Bureau numbers assigned to the PBJ-1H aircraft were 35250 through 35297 and 88872 through 89071.

The recess through which the 75mm gun barrel protruded constituted a blast tube. The lower half of the nose was fixed, whereas the top half was hinged at its top rear, forming a hood, as on the B-25G. To the far right is the slab of 3/8-inch armor plate that gave the pilot some side protection from flak; this plate was not repeated on the right side. (Stan Piet collection)

The B-25H-1 was equipped with two .50-caliber gun packs on the right side of the fuselage. With the B-25H-5, two gun packs were also installed on the left side, as seen here. With four gun packs on the sides of the aircraft and with the dorsal turret firing to the front, the B-25H could concentrate ten .50-caliber machine guns and a 75mm gun on a target. (National Museum of the United States Air Force)

In this B-25H nose, the .50-caliber magazines have been removed from their trays. The two center machine guns are positioned slightly higher than the two outboard guns. When they were installed in the aircraft, the gun barrels were wrapped to protect them from the elements. Between the two center guns is a gun camera. (National Archives)

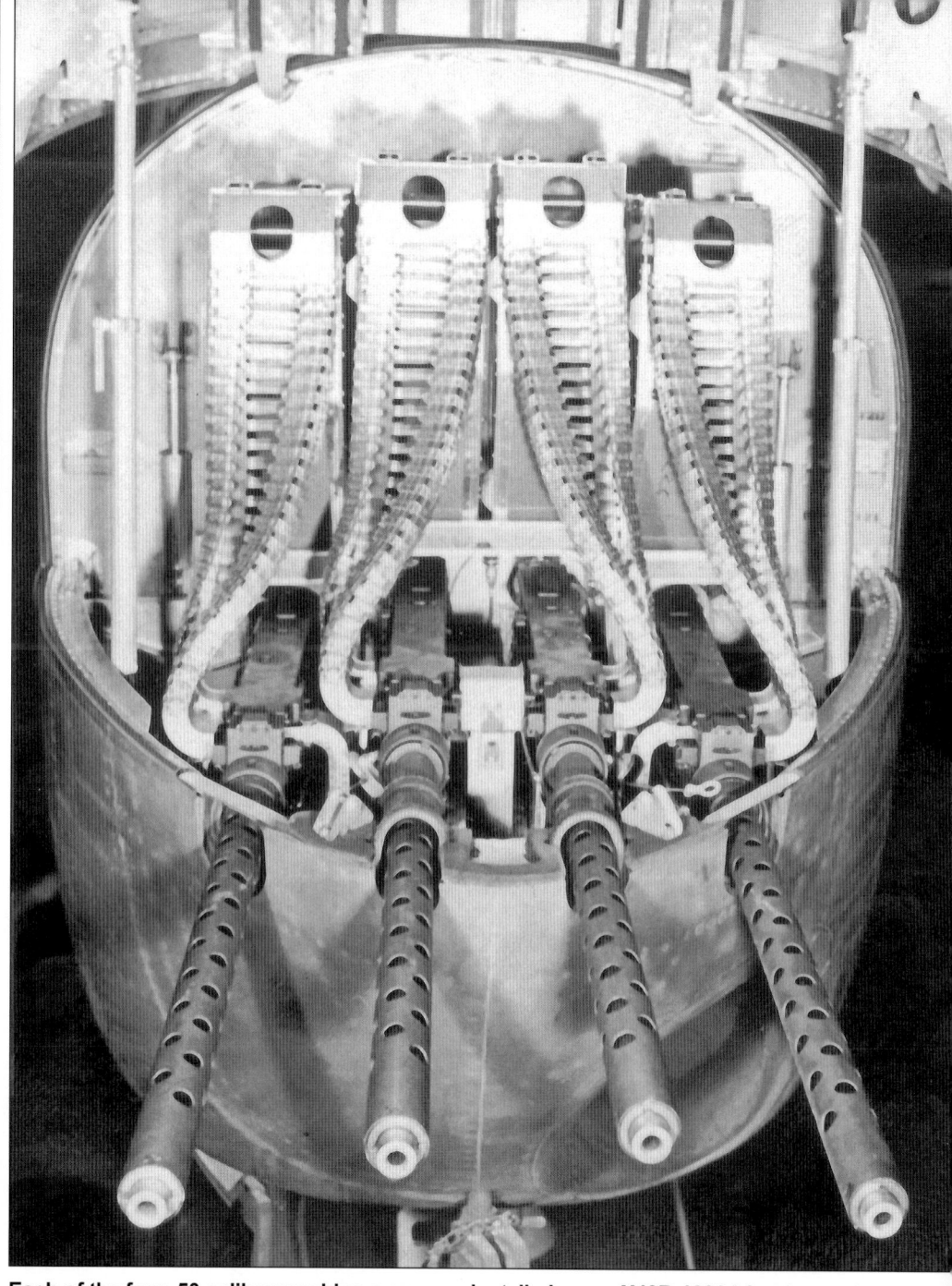

Each of the four .50-caliber machine guns was installed on an X43B-10934 front mount and a Type A4 rear post. The guns were fired electrically by the pilot and electrically charged. Above and aft of the guns, four 400-round ammunition magazines supplied the guns via flex chutes. Two spring-loaded struts held the hood open. (National Archives)

55

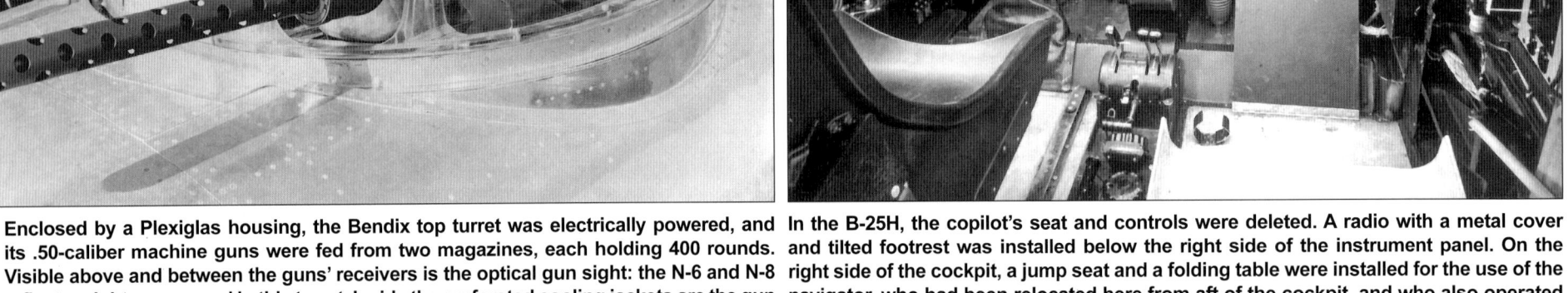

Enclosed by a Plexiglas housing, the Bendix top turret was electrically powered, and its .50-caliber machine guns were fed from two magazines, each holding 400 rounds. Visible above and between the guns' receivers is the optical gun sight: the N-6 and N-8 reflector sights were used in this turret. Inside the perforated cooling jackets are the gun barrels. (National Museum of the United States Air Force)

The pilot's area of the cockpit of a B-25H is viewed from the right. The console to the right in the photo contained controls for the throttles and propellers. Across the top center are the command transmitter and receiver controls. The black box at the center of the photo is the bomb-control panel: the B-25H pilot also served as bombardier. (National Archives)

In the B-25H, the copilot's seat and controls were deleted. A radio with a metal cover and tilted footrest was installed below the right side of the instrument panel. On the right side of the cockpit, a jump seat and a folding table were installed for the use of the navigator, who had been relocated here from aft of the cockpit, and who also operated the cannon. (National Archives)

This is a pilot's view of the navigator's station on the right side of a B-25H cockpit. On the side wall at the top center is the radio-compass control box. The light-colored fixture next to it is the navigator's intercom control box. To the far right is the front end of the navigator's jump seat. A folding table usually installed to the top right is missing. (National Archives)

B-25Hs are under construction at North American Aviation's plant in Inglewood, California. By this point in the B-25's development, the prominent fairings over the two oil-cooler air outlets on the right wing had been deleted, and these outlets now were fully exposed, like the two outlets on the left wing. (USAF)

Civilians of all ages tour the Inglewood plant, with nearly complete B-25Hs lined up along the side. The Mitchell's skin was composed of Alclad sheeting, a corrosion-resistant composite of high-purity aluminum surfaces bonded to an aluminum alloy core. The ailerons, elevators, and rudders were covered with doped fabric. (USAF)

In the foreground is the first B-25H-5, serial number 43-4405. Pronounced discoloration from the blasts of the .50-caliber package machine guns is visible on the side of the fuselage. Prolonged firing of the package guns could distort and damage the skin to the front of the muzzles, so blast shields were often installed over the skin in these areas. (DAABMA)

B-25H-5 serial number 43-4550 speeds along a coast. In addition to the gun camera and the left-side .50-caliber gun packages, the B-25H-5 saw the introduction of an electric bomb-control system. The two small "blisters" on the top deck aft of the upper turret were armored bullet deflectors, to prevent the guns in that turret from shooting-up the tail turret. (USAF)

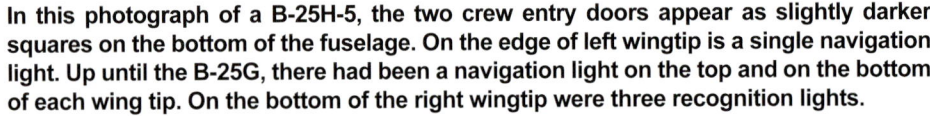

In this photograph of a B-25H-5, the two crew entry doors appear as slightly darker squares on the bottom of the fuselage. On the edge of left wingtip is a single navigation light. Up until the B-25G, there had been a navigation light on the top and on the bottom of each wing tip. On the bottom of the right wingtip were three recognition lights.

Bombs rain down all around this B-25H of the 12th Bomb Group on a 23 July 1944 raid on Myitkyina, Burma (now Myanmar). Although the B-25H is closely identified with the war in the Pacific, the model also served elsewhere. The 12th Bomb Group flew the B-25H in both the Mediterranean and the China-Burma-India Theaters. (Stan Piet collection)

A B-25H-1 whose partially visible tail number appears to be 34361 is about to receive a tow from a small tractor, probably at North American's Inglewood plant. A number of curved, colored strips of material are intricately attached to the aircraft; their purpose is unclear, but they may have been some sort of test indicators. (USAF)

B-25H-10 serial number 43-5052 of the 12th Bomb Group refuels at Meiktila, Burma (now Myanmar), as crewmen ready the bomber for its next mission. Upgrades designed into the B-25H-10 include a redesigned layout of the pilot's instruments, an enlarged life-raft compartment, and a revised control cable for the brake system. (Stan Piet collection)

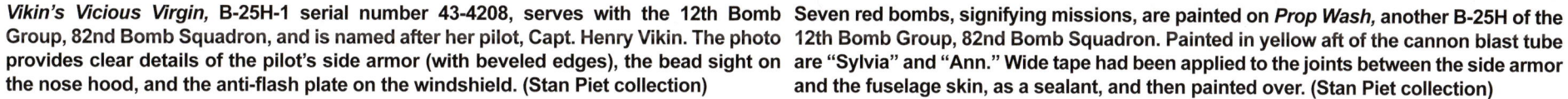

Vikin's Vicious Virgin, B-25H-1 serial number 43-4208, serves with the 12th Bomb Group, 82nd Bomb Squadron, and is named after her pilot, Capt. Henry Vikin. The photo provides clear details of the pilot's side armor (with beveled edges), the bead sight on the nose hood, and the anti-flash plate on the windshield. (Stan Piet collection)

After serving in the Mediterranean, in early 1944 the 12th Bomb Group was reassigned to the China-Burma-India (CBI) Theater, where one of the group's B-25H-10s, *Silver Streak,* of the 83rd Bomb Squadron, was photographed. The waist machine gun protrudes from a square cutout in the lower aft corner of the window. (Stan Piet collection)

Seven red bombs, signifying missions, are painted on *Prop Wash,* another B-25H of the 12th Bomb Group, 82nd Bomb Squadron. Painted in yellow aft of the cannon blast tube are "Sylvia" and "Ann." Wide tape had been applied to the joints between the side armor and the fuselage skin, as a sealant, and then painted over. (Stan Piet collection)

The 12th Bomb Group was renowned for its risqué nose art, another example of which was *Eatin' Kitty,* a B-25H-10 attached to the 82nd Bomb Squadron. This bomber, serial number 43-4909, reportedly served with the 12th Bomb Group in the Mediterranean, and by June 1944 it was based in Karachi, India (now Pakistan). (Stan Piet collection)

Bones, the 1,000th and final B-25H to leave North American's Inglewood plant, serial number 43-5104, received a special commemoration when employees who had worked on the bomber were allowed to autograph her. Although often listed as assigned to the 81st Bomb Squadron, she actually served with the 12th Bomb Group, 82nd Bomb Squadron, arriving in the CBI Theater in December 1944. (Stan Piet collection)

Mechanics service *Bones* at an advanced airfield in India. Written willy-nilly over almost every available exterior surface are the initials, first names, surnames, nicknames, and full names of hundreds of employees of North American Aviation as well as other graffiti. Also visible on the nose of the B-25H-10 is the faint evidence of a set of painted-on shark's teeth. (Stan Piet collection)

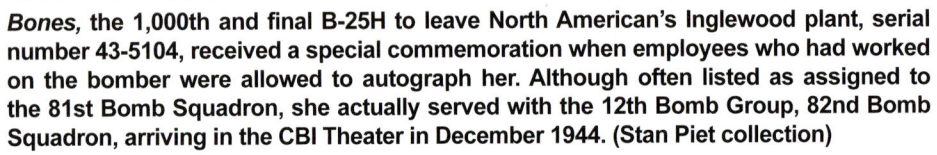

From this perspective, the shark's teeth on the right side of *Bones* are more prominent. The aircraft's nickname is written in bold block letters on the side of the fuselage. In the background, below the right wing, a crewman is using a wooden packing crate as a work bench for servicing two of the aircraft's .50-caliber machine guns. (National Archives)

Bones poses for a formal portrait. During the final days of World War II, this aircraft suffered a midair collision with a vulture, which flew through the windshield. The bomber landed safely, but it flew no further combat missions. In this photograph, the machine gun barrels are wrapped with protective covers of paper and tape. (National Archives)

PBJ-1H

The PBJ-1H is the USMC version of the B-25H. The Marines received 236 of this model and employed them primarily in the ground-attack, anti-shipping, and coastal-patrol roles. PBJ-1Hs were drawn from stocks of B-25H-5s and B-25H-10s, with the vast majority representing B-25H-10s. One PBJ-1H, bureau number 35227, even conducted successful aircraft carrier trials aboard the USS *Shangri La,* although there was no subsequent effort to base PBJs on aircraft carriers operationally. Here, PBJ-1Hs on a flight line display a three-color camouflage scheme, most likely of non-specular sea blue on the upper surfaces, intermediate blue on the sides, and insignia white on the lower surfaces. (Stan Piet collection)

A factory-fresh PBJ-1H, its gun barrels still wrapped, flies over California mountains. Although, as with many PBJs, a prominent bureau number was not painted on this aircraft, the number 818 was lightly chalked on the fuselage below the front corner of the pilot's side armor plate. Aft of that plate, stenciled in black is the aircraft's data block. (USAF)

The same PBJ-1H as seen in the above photo flies over the Southern California coast. Except for the national insignia, markings have not been added to this PBJ-1H. Typically, operational PBJs did not wear much by way of markings, aside from individual aircraft numbers and, in some cases, letter codes signifying the home base. (USAF)

A new PBJ-1H appears to be undergoing final adjustments. The .50-caliber machine guns' cooling jackets are carefully wrapped, and the ammunition flex chutes are draped over the nose section. The small object on the fuselage below and aft of the 75mm cannon blast tube was a ram-air vent for extracting ammunition fumes from the nose. (Stan Piet collection)

B-25J

At North American Aviation's Kansas City plant in 1943, production shifted from the B-25D to a new model that would become by far the most numerous model of the Mitchell: the B-25J. From the front of the cockpit to the tail of the aircraft, the B-25J was virtually identical to the B-25H, but instead of the snubbed gun nose of the H model, a bombardier's nose similar to that of the B-25D was installed. Later, an all-metal nose containing eight .50-caliber machine guns would be introduced as a factory installation or as a kit for assembly in the field. Seen here is a B-25J-30 factory painted in camouflage and insignia for delivery to the Soviet Air Force under the Lend-Lease program. (Stan Piet collection)

Beginning in December 1943, North American began producing the B-25J, which remained in production into August 1945. The B-25J was built exclusively at North American's Kansas City facility.

For the bulk of the production, the glass nose of the early Mitchells returned, as did the dual-control pilot-copilot cockpit configuration. Strangely, although no J model was cannon-armed, the flash shield remained on the pilot's windshield.

Initially, the waist, tail, and upper turret mountings were the same as those found on late model Hs. Beginning with 44-31491, however, an M-8A tail gun mount with K-10 lead-computing sight replaced the earlier M-7 mount.

During the course of production, several minor changes were made in gun sights, electrical and hydraulic apparatus. Also, new armored seats for the pilot and copilot were devised and installed, the flexible nose gun mounting was raised, and the rear of the top turret was reinforced.

Although no longer armed with the 75mm cannon, the Mitchell continued to serve in the strafer role. Toward that end, 1,000 kits were produced that permitted the installation of a solid nose in place of the greenhouse bombardier's position. This solid nose housed a whopping eight .50-caliber machine guns. Reportedly, some of these kits were installed on aircraft even before they left the factory.

The U.S. Navy owned 244 of the B-25J, which it called the PBJ-1J. The Royal Air Force took delivery of 314 of the machines, dubbing them Mitchell III. A few other countries received considerably lesser numbers of the airplane.

The same newly minted B-25J-25 is viewed from the opposite side. The painted metal panel on the rear of the top turret is a strengthener introduced with the B-25J-20. The installation of the second static .50-caliber machine gun in the nose and the raising of the flex nose gun by four inches were also changes introduced in the B-25J-20. (Stan Piet collection)

This B-25J-25 is another aircraft produced at the Kansas City plant already painted and marked for Soviet service. The bright objects on the ends of the barrels of the top turret and side-pack .50-caliber machine guns are blast deflectors, intended to divert the muzzle blast away from the aircraft; otherwise the blast could damage the aircraft's skin. (Stan Piet collection)

A B-25J of the 12th Bomb Group is parked on a hardstand made of matting at the USAAF airfield at Fenny, India (now in Bangladesh). The individual aircraft number, 51, is painted in black on the tail. On B-25Js with the clear bombardier's nose, the pilot also retained a low-level bomb sight and bomb controls similar to the arrangement in the B-25H. (Stan Piet collection)

Oh Dee Whiz! served with the 12th Bomb Group. Details are visible of the flexible nose gun and the adapter on which it is mounted. Two fixed .50-caliber machine guns protrude through the lower right side of the nose; these were fed from large ammunition magazines on the right side of the bombardier's compartment.

The B-25J nicknamed *Pin-up Girl* was yet another of the many Mitchells of the 12th Bomb Group that sported risqué nose art. Directly above the bulldog's head is the escape hatch built into the side of the bombardier's clear enclosure. Because of its proximity to the propeller, this hatch was for use only on the ground, with the engines stopped. (Stan Piet collection)

Ground crewmen use a Jeep and trailer as a scaffold to work on a late Mitchell's tail turret. Aluminum side panels were removable for better access to the gun mount and ammunition feeds. One crewman has removed the escape panel of the canopy and is standing up through the hatch. Also present is the canvas cover for the gun mount. (Stan Piet collection)

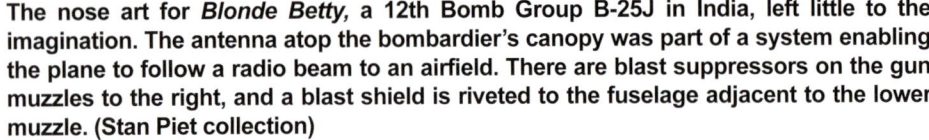

The nose art for *Blonde Betty,* a 12th Bomb Group B-25J in India, left little to the imagination. The antenna atop the bombardier's canopy was part of a system enabling the plane to follow a radio beam to an airfield. There are blast suppressors on the gun muzzles to the right, and a blast shield is riveted to the fuselage adjacent to the lower muzzle. (Stan Piet collection)

These B-25Js have the eight-gun solid noses, and painted on the noses are black panthers' heads, the symbol of the 338th Bomb Group's 822nd Bomb Squadron. The closest bomber has the number 377 as well as the serial number painted in yellow on the vertical tail. Similarly, the lower part of the tail is painted as a unit identification sign.

My Duchess, a B-25J of the 345th Bomb Group, 499th Bomb Squadron "Bats out of Hell," was modified into a strafer aircraft by having the clear panels of the nose painted and extra fixed .50-caliber machine guns installed therein. Painted on the batwing design were symbols for eight enemy ships sunk. A canvas cover is fastened over the top turret.

Navigator-bombardier Capt. Milton Molakides poses in the pilot's seat of a B-25J of the 341st Bomb Group, 491st Bomb Squadron, nicknamed the "Ringer Squadron," as reflected on the insignia appearing on the pilot's side armor plate. The 491st was a China-Burma-India squadron, serving in-theater from early 1943 to the end of the war. (Stan Piet collection)

The Royal Air Force secured some 300 B-25J medium bombers, redesignating them Mitchell III and assigning them RAF numbers HD346-HD400, KJ561-KJ800, and KP308-KP328 (some of these were diverted to Canada and the USAAF). Two other Commonwealth countries, Australia and Canada, also flew B-25Js during World War II.

These two B-25Js (including one with an eight-gun nose) of the 41st Bomb Group, 47th Bomb Squadron, are preparing for a mission from Okinawa to Sasebo Harbor, Kyushu, Japan, at the end of July 1945. The bombers have externally mounted GT-1 glide torpedoes with wings and stabilizers, allowing them to be dropped at a greater than normal distance from an enemy ship. The closer aircraft is named *Luki-Bets*. (National Archives)

A ground crewman removes protective tubes from the eight .50-caliber machine guns in the nose of a B-25J of the 41st Bomb Group on Okinawa on 30 June 1945. The aircraft was about to participate in the first B-25 raid on the Japanese home islands since the 1942 Doolittle Raid. Both of the access doors to the nose-gun compartment are raised. (National Archives)

67

Within five minutes after this B-25J of the 38th Bomb Group, 823rd Bomb Squadron, landed at Clark Field, Luzon, after a mission on 17 May 1945, armorers were quickly preparing it for another mission. The boxes stacked on the scaffold are .50-caliber ammunition magazines that had been removed from the left side of the nose gun bay. (National Archives)

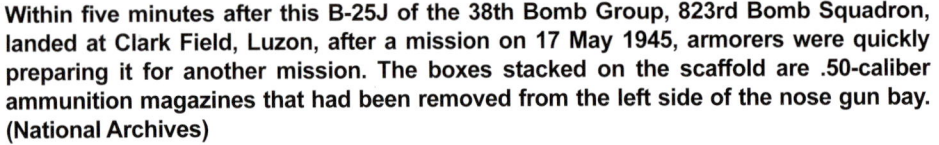

The solid noses of the B-25J gunships of the 405th Bomb Squadron "Green Dragons" of the 38th Bomb Group offered plenty of space for scary renderings of dragons. The squadron was based at a succession of airfields in the Southwest Pacific and Okinawa. The tail number of the second aircraft in line, 430921, identifies it as a B-25J-30. (National Museum of the United States Air Force)

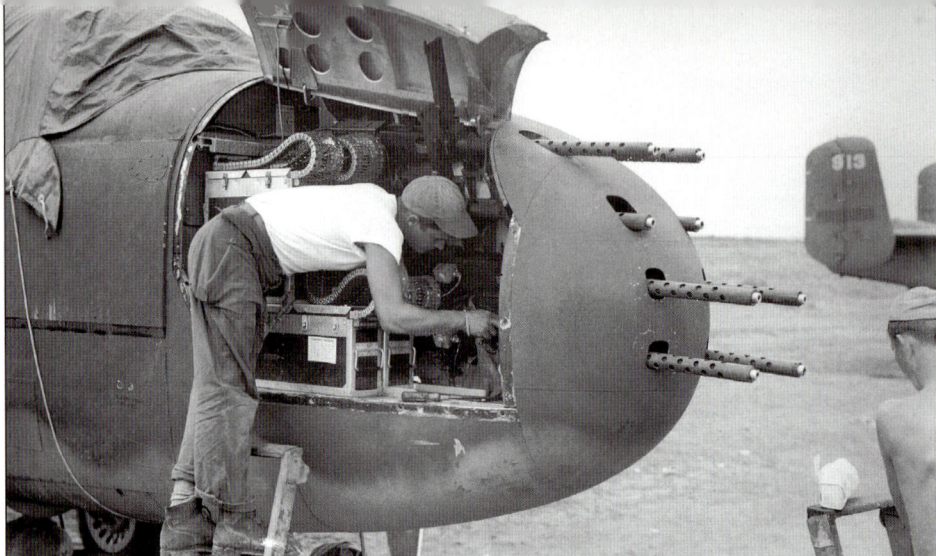

A ground crewman adjusts a .50-caliber machine gun in a solid-nosed B-25J of the 500th Bomb Group at Clark Field, Luzon, in May 1945. Ammunition boxes were arranged on the outer sides of the guns, four per side. Since a copilot was included in the B-25J, an external armor plate was attached to the right side of the cockpit as well as the left. (National Archives)

Mabels Stable was a B-25J gunship serving with the 498th Bomb Squadron "Falcons" of the 345th Bomb Group "Air Apaches" in the Pacific Theater. Weatherproof protective sleeves are fitted over the eight .50-caliber machine gun barrels. The anti-flash panel on the left side of the windshield was a vestige from the B-25G and B-25H gunships. (Stan Piet collection)

Bottoms Up, a B-25J-5 serial number 43-27900, has its landing gear lowered as it comes in for a landing. By March 1944 this aircraft was assigned to the 340th Bomb Group, 486th Bomb Squadron, based at Gaudo, Italy. It featured an unusual mix of colors, including what appear to be zinc chromate horizontal stabilizers and engine nacelle. (Stan Piet collection)

A B-25J gunship is photographed at a base in the Pacific. The square metal panel on the rear of the turret is the strengthener introduced with the B-25J-20. As can be seen in photos of other B-25J gunships, when the noses were painted in camouflage or with art work, the outlines of the access doors to the nose gun compartments were very indistinct. (Stan Piet collection)

One of the B-25J gunships of the 38th Bomb Group, 405th Bomb Squadron, is parked at a Pacific air field. The nose sports one of the distinctive dragon designs characteristic of that squadron. Red covers are fitted over at least four of the fixed .50-caliber machine guns in the nose, and specially fitted covers are secured over the canopy and top turret.

Using a portable tripod crane on a Marston matting hardstand, ground crewmen unpack a Wright Cyclone engine alongside a B-25J. Hard use wore engines out, so overhauls and complete engine replacements were part of the job of keeping these bombers flying. The lower part of the B-25J's vertical tail appears to be painted white. (Stan Piet collection)

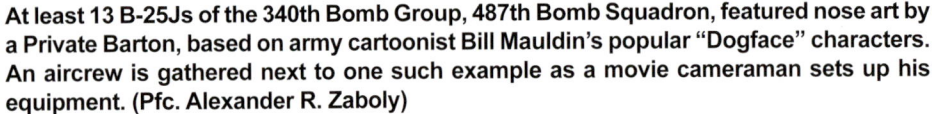

At least 13 B-25Js of the 340th Bomb Group, 487th Bomb Squadron, featured nose art by a Private Barton, based on army cartoonist Bill Mauldin's popular "Dogface" characters. An aircrew is gathered next to one such example as a movie cameraman sets up his equipment. (Pfc. Alexander R. Zaboly)

That's All Brother was a B-25J of the 340th Bomb Group, 489th Bomb Squadron, on Corsica. Bomb symbols for 27 missions are stenciled on the nose, and the names of the pilot and crew chief are in the light-colored placard above the aircraft's nickname. This aircraft later crashed in a runway accident after flying 38 missions. (Pfc. Alexander R. Zaboly)

Two ground crewmen of the 340th Bomb Group on Corsica in 1944 make adjustments to the top turret of a B-25J with the Plexiglas enclosure removed. The .50-caliber ammunition belts came up from the their magazines and then made a 90° turn over the rollers and into the feeds on the machine gun receivers. (Pfc. Alexander R. Zaboly)

Movie cameramen use platforms on Chevrolet panel trucks to film a B-25 as it takes off from Edwards Air Force Base, Muroc, California, around early 1954. The aircraft has the number BD-123 on the fuselage. After World War II, hundreds of B-25s were modified for the services into trainers, passenger transports, and special-purpose aircraft. (National Archives)

The U.S. Navy acquired 244 B-25Js produced at North American's Kansas City plant, delivering them to the U.S. Marine Corps and redesignating them the PBJ-1J. A number of these aircraft were fitted with radomes on their noses or on their starboard wingtips. In addition, several PBJ-1Js were modified to carry externally two Tiny Tim rockets. (National Museum of Naval Aviation)

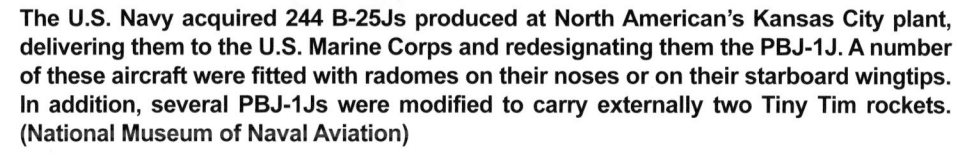

The same PBJ-1J shown in the photograph at left is viewed here from above. The three-color paint scheme consisted of non-specular sea blue on the upper surfaces, intermediate blue on the sides, and insignia white on the bottom. Intermediate blue is painted on the upper leading edges of the wings and the horizontal stabilizers. (National Museum of Naval Aviation)

The same PBJ-1J in the above photo is viewed here from below. On the underside of the starboard wingtip are three recognition lights: red, green, and amber, from front to rear. Three static dischargers are visible on the outboard part of each aileron. The national insignia on the fuselage covers all signs of the circular escape hatch (a B-25H addition) except the very bottom. (National Museum of Naval Aviation)

This USMC PBJ-1J on Okinawa in September 1945 has a radome mounted on the starboard wing. All of the .50-caliber machine guns have been removed except the two in the top turret. Openings for two fixed guns are visible on the clear nose. On the underside of the wing are four pairs of zero-length launchers for 5-inch HVAR rockets. (National Museum of Naval Aviation)

After World War II, the U.S. Air Force continued to fly some B-25s, including trainer versions, such as this TB-25J numbered BD-914 and reportedly photographed at the USAF Test Pilot School at Edwards Air Force Base, California, in 1954. The trainers were disarmed, modified to accommodate student pilots, and painted in special colors. This, and personnel transport, would be the final use of the B-25 by the US military. (National Museum of the United States Air Force)